kitty knits

projects for cats and their people

DONNA DRUCHUNAS

Martingale®
& COMPANY

Kitty Knits: Projects for Cats and Their People
© 2008 by Donna Druchunas

Martingale®
& C O M P A N Y

Martingale & Company®
20205 144th Ave. NE
Woodinville, WA 98072-8478 USA
www.martingale-pub.com

Printed in China
13 12 11 10 09 08   8 7 6 5 4 3 2 1

Library of Congress Cataloging-in-Publication Data
Library of Congress Control Number: 2007036797

ISBN: 978-1-56477-838-3

credits

President & CEO   Tom Wierzbicki

Publisher   Jane Hamada

Editorial Director   Mary V. Green

Managing Editor   Tina Cook

Developmental Editor   Karen Costello Soltys

Technical Editor   Ursula Reikes

Copy Editor   Liz McGehee

Design Director   Stan Green

Assistant Design Director   Regina Girard

Illustrator   Robin Strobel

Cover & Text Designer   Shelly Garrison

Photographer   Brent Kane

mission statement

Dedicated to providing quality products and service to inspire creativity.

dedication

For my sister June and her feline friends:
Oliver, Bob, George, Peter, Chloe,
Samantha, Stewart, Greg,
Bonnie, and Clyde.

acknowledgments

Many thanks to everyone who helped me take my idea and turn it into a book:

To Susan McBride, who made sketches that I turned into knitting charts for the Needle-Felted Cat Bed with Needle-Felted Mouse, the Felted Carpet Bag, the Felted Appliqué Pillow, and the Felted Cat Doorstop.

To Joanne Turcotte at Plymouth Yarns, for generously providing all the yarns for the projects.

To everyone at Martingale & Company whose hands touched these pages: Tami Aderrab, Tina Cook, Mary Green, and Karen Soltys—thank you for taking my vision and making it come to life. Special thanks to my editor, Ursula Reikes, for her technical expertise. Thank-you to photographer Brent Kane for showing off my projects to their best advantage, and illustrator Robin Strobel, who took my rough charts and drawings and created the final illustrations that you see on these pages. Thank-you to Shelly Garrison for coming up with a fun and pleasant design.

I used several software programs to create the charts in this book, including Stitch & Motif Maker from software4knitting.com for Fair-Isle charts, Knit Visualizer from knitfoundry.com for lace and texture charts, and knitPro from microrevolt.org for intarsia charts.

Without the test knitters who helped me make the sample projects, I never would have been able to finish this book. Special thanks to Judy Alexander, Kris Bart, Joyce Druchunas, Helen Marshall, Caitlin Moore, Debbie O'Neill, and Ingrid Ulbrich. You are all part of this book.

contents

introduction

 Cats love knitting. They love to play with yarn. They love to dump everything out of a knitting basket. They love to chew on wooden knitting needles. And they love to sleep on anything knitted.

If you look around a cat lover's house, office, or car, you'll undoubtedly find a plethora of objects decorated with pictures of cats. From mugs, place mats, and afghans around the house; to calendars, computer wallpaper, and figurines at work; to pillows, stickers, and stuffed animals in the car, cat lovers surround themselves with pictures of their beloved animals.

Kitty Knits gives us a chance to celebrate our love of cats through knitting. With projects for cats, people, and the home, this book will be a welcome addition to the knitting library of all knitters with cats in the family. Inside these pages you will find projects for knitters of all skill levels. Even if you only know how to cast on, bind off, and do the knit stitch, there are projects here you can complete. For expert knitters, I've included several projects to give you a challenge. And for those of you in between, I've included many intermediate projects and a section on knitting, finishing, and embellishment techniques to help you expand your skills.

So, what are you waiting for? Get out those needles and cast on a project for your feline friends!

felted eyelash **cat bed** with **cushion**

this furry cat bed is knit from wool yarn combined with eyelash yarn. The bed and pillow are knit flat in garter stitch, so you don't even need to know how to purl. After the knitting is finished, the bed is thrown into the washing machine to felt it. The pillow is stuffed with quilt batting. What could be more luxurious for that pampered feline friend?

SKILL LEVEL:

Beginner ◼☐☐☐

FINISHED MEASUREMENTS

Cushion: 8" x 15"

Bed: Approx 18" long x 13" wide x 3" high (after felting)

Exact size is determined during felting.

MATERIALS

A 5 balls of Galway Worsted from Plymouth Yarn (100% wool; 210 yds; 100 g), color 150 (red) (4)

B 2 balls of Colorlash* from Plymouth Yarn (100% polyester; 220 yds; 50 g), color 8 (red) (1)

Size 13 (9 mm) needles or size to obtain gauge for bed

Size 8 (5 mm) needles or size to obtain gauge for cushion

Tapestry needle

Polyester fiberfill for stuffing

*Warning: If you have kittens or cats that eat strings, do not make this bed with eyelash yarn. Instead use a faux-fur yarn that does not have any long strings. Cats can sustain serious intestinal injuries and even die from eating strings.

GAUGE

Bed: Approx 8 sts = 4" in garter st using 2 strands of A and larger needles (before felting)

Exact gauge is not critical. Make sure your stitches are open and airy for felting.

Cushion: 16 sts = 4" in garter st using 1 strand of A and smaller needles

GARTER STITCH

Knit every st in every row.

BED

With larger needles and 1 strand each of A and B held tog, CO 48 sts.

Work in garter st until piece measures 8".

Cut B and add a second strand of A. Work in garter st until wool section is approx 24" square.

Cut second strand of A yarn and add strand of B. Work in garter st until eyelash section measures 8".

BO all sts.

Turn the piece on its side. Using 1 strand each of A and B held tog, working along plain wool section, pick up 1 st for each garter ridge.

Work in garter st until eyelash section measures 8". BO all sts.

Rep on other side of wool center section.

Finishing

Weave in ends. Sew corner seams so piece forms a box shape. Felt the bed piece according to instructions on page 76.

Pinch each corner of the bed and use 1 strand of A to tie it with a knot to help keep the shape. Bury the yarn ends inside the corner of the bed.

CUSHION

With smaller needles and 1 strand of A, CO 60 sts.

Work in garter st until pillow measures 16".

BO all sts.

Weave in ends.

Finishing

Fold pillow in half and sew side seams. Stuff lightly with fiberfill and sew top seam. Pinch pillow in center and tack with a couple of sewing stitches if desired. Bury the remaining yarn ends inside the pillow.

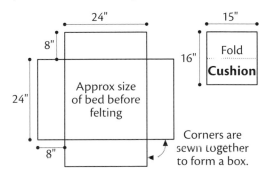

bull's-eye **cat bed**

his cuddly cat bed is fun to make! It's knit in the round, with fur and wool yarn forming the sides, and two colors of wool yarn striped on the bottom. Stuffed with quilt batting, it's as soft as it is pretty.

SKILL LEVEL

Intermediate ◖◼◼◻

FINISHED MEASUREMENTS

Approx 13" in diameter x 4" high (when stuffed)

MATERIALS

A 2 balls of Encore Worsted from Plymouth Yarn (75% acrylic, 25% wool; 200 yds; 100 g), color 1203 (tan) 🄰

B 2 balls of Encore Worsted from Plymouth Yarn, color 514 (blue) 🄰

C 2 balls of Flash from Plymouth Yarn (100% nylon; 190 yds; 50 g), color 992 (tan) 🄰

Size 9 (5.5 mm) circular needle (20" long) or size to obtain gauge

Size 9 (5.5 mm) double-pointed needles

10 stitch markers (1 a different color for beg of rnd)

Tapestry needle

½ yard of quilt batting, approx ½" thick

GAUGE

14 sts = 4" in St st with 2 strands of A or B held tog

STOCKINETTE STITCH (CIRCULAR)

Knit every st in every rnd.

INSTRUCTIONS

Bed is worked from the sides inward to the center bottom.

Sides

With 1 strand of A and 2 strands of C held tog, CO 110 sts. Pm and join to knit in the rnd, being careful not to twist sts. Work in St st until piece measures 10".

Bottom

Cut C. Add second strand of A. Knit 1 rnd, pm after every 11th st—10 sections with 11 sts each. Use a different colored marker for beg of rnd.

Beg stripe patt and AT SAME TIME work dec rnds as indicated below:

> Work 4 rnds with 2 strands of B.
>
> Work 2 rnds with 2 strands of A.

DECREASE ROUNDS

Rnd 1 (dec rnd): (Knit to 2 sts before marker, K2tog) around.

Rnds 2 and 3: Knit.

Maintaining stripe patt, rep rnds 1–3 a total of 4 times, then work rnd 1 every other rnd until 2 sts rem in each section. Change to dpns when sts no longer fit on circular needle.

K2tog around.

Cut yarn, leaving a 6" tail. Run tail through rem sts and fasten off.

False Bottom

With 2 strands of B, CO 110 sts. Join, pm, and work as for bottom of bed without changing colors.

FINISHING

Weave in ends.

Cut a piece of batting the size to go around the sides of the bed. Fold the fur edge down like a cuff on the outside of bed. Put batting between layers and sew CO edge to first row of knitting without fur.

Cut a piece of batting the size of the bed bottom and cover it with the false bottom, RS facing out. Sew the false bottom to the CO edge of the fur sides.

Weave in ends and bury inside bed.

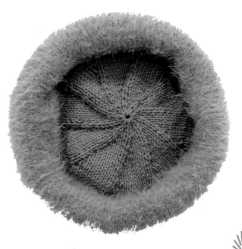

felted goldfish cat place mat

do you ever get tired of your cat spilling food all over your clean floor? This place mat for your cat couldn't be more fun to make. It is knit in the round, so you don't have to purl with two colors. After you finish knitting, you cut the tube open and felt it. Crochet edging adds the perfect finishing touch.

SKILL LEVEL
Intermediate ◀■■▭

FINISHED MEASUREMENTS
Approx 17" x 15" (after felting)

Exact size is determined during felting.

MATERIALS
Tweed from Plymouth Yarn (100% virgin lamb's wool; 109 yds; 50 g)

MC 2 balls of color 5317 (blue)

A 2 balls of color 5324 (aqua)

B 1 ball of color 5327 (orange)

Size 10 (6 mm) circular needle (20" long) or size to obtain gauge

Stitch holder or spare needle

Extra needle for three-needle bind off

Size 7 (4.5mm.) crochet hook

Approx ½ yard of nonslip rubber rug backing

Sewing needle and matching thread

GAUGE
Approx 12 sts and 18 rows = 4" in St st (before felting)

Check your gauge over solid St st and over the color chart. Some knitters need to use a larger needle to get the same gauge in the color knitting.

STOCKINETTE STITCH (CIRCULAR)
Knit every st in every rnd.

INSTRUCTIONS
Be sure to weave the colors after every 1 or 2 sts so there are no long floats because the floats shrink more than the sts during felting (see page 76).

Half Place Mat (Make 2)
With A, CO 74 sts. Wrap yarn around needle 10 times. Join to knit in the rnd, being careful not to twist sts.

NOTE: At beg of each rnd, wrap yarn around right needle 10 times. When you are working with 2 colors in a row, wrap both yarns tog. Knit the first and last sts of each row through the back loop. When you are working with 2 colors in a row, knit this st using both colors tog.

Work 4 rows in St st.

Work all rows of goldfish border chart, working first and last stitches as mentioned in note above.

Cont with MC, work in St st for another 6".

Do not BO. Place sts on a stitch holder or a spare needle.

Cut place mat open in the middle of the wrapped yarn. Take 2 strands of cut ends and tie them tog with the knot as close to the knitted piece as possible. Rep until all ends have been tied in pairs.

FINISHING
With RS tog, join the 2 pieces with three-needle bind off.

Tie ends in knots as for cut pieces.

Felt according to the instructions on page 76. Cut off yarn ends close to the edge of the felted piece. Don't worry; it won't unravel.

Crochet Edging

With crochet hook and MC, work 2 rnds of sc (see page 78) and 1 rnd of crab st (see page 78) around entire edge of place mat, working 3 sts in each corner st.

Fasten off. Weave in ends.

Nonslip Backing

Cut the nonslip backing material to the size of the place mat. Fold ½" under on each edge of backing for a hem. With sewing needle and thread, sew backing to WS of place mat.

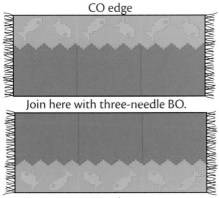

Cats Sleep Anywhere
by Eleanor Farjeon

Cats sleep anywhere, any table, any chair.

Top of piano, window-ledge, in the middle, on the edge.

Open drawer, empty shoe, anybody's lap will do.

Fitted in a cardboard box, in the cupboard with your frocks.

Anywhere! They don't care!

Cats sleep anywhere.

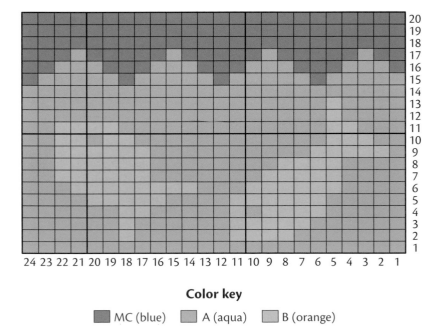

CO edge

Join here with three-needle BO.

CO edge

Color key

■ MC (blue)   ■ A (aqua)   ■ B (orange)

felted **catnip mice**

need a great stocking stuffer for cat-loving friends? This catnip mouse is knit back and forth with bobble ears and an I-cord tail. Stuffed with fiberfill and a touch of catnip, this little mouse will drive your furry friends crazy with delight.

SKILL LEVEL

Easy ◼◼☐☐

FINISHED MEASUREMENTS

Approx 3" to 4" long (after felting)

Exact size is determined during felting.

MATERIALS

1 ball of Galway Worsted from Plymouth Yarn (100% wool; 210 yds; 100 g), assorted colors (**4**) (One ball of yarn will make several mice.)

2 size 10½ (6.5 mm) double-pointed needles or size to obtain gauge

Tapestry needle

1 yard of black embroidery floss

Sharp embroidery needle

Sewing needle and matching thread

Polyester fiberfill for stuffing

Catnip

GAUGE

Approx 12 sts = 4" in St st before felting

Exact gauge is not critical. Make sure your stitches are open and airy for felting.

STOCKINETTE STITCH

Knit RS rows; purl WS rows.

BOBBLE

Row 1 (RS): (K1, P1, K1, P1, K1) in same st—5 sts made. Turn.

Row 2: P5. Turn.

Row 3: K5. Turn.

Row 4: P5. Turn.

Row 5: K1, K2tog, pass first st over as in binding off, K2tog, pass previous st over—1 st rem in bobble.

Bobble finished.

INSTRUCTIONS

The mouse is worked from the tail to the head.

Tail

CO 3 sts.

Work 3-st I-cord for 3½" (see page 74).

Body

Start working back and forth.

Row 1 (RS): CO 1 st, knit to end of row—4 sts.

Row 2 (and all WS rows): Purl.

Row 3: K1f&b of each st—8 sts.

Row 5: K1f&b of each st—16 sts.

Row 7: (K1, K1f&b), rep across 24 sts.

Work even in St st on 24 sts for 2½". End by working a WS row.

Head

Row 1 (RS): (K4, K2tog) across—20 sts.

Row 2 (and all WS rows): Purl.

Row 3: K7, make bobble, K4, make bobble, K7.

Row 5: (K3, K2tog) across—16 sts.

Row 7: (K2 K2tog) across— 12 sts.

Row 9: (K1, K2tog) across—8 sts.

Row 11: K2tog across—4 sts.

Row 13: K2tog twice—2 sts.

BO.

FINISHING

Sew seam, leaving approx 1" open for stuffing.

Felt mouse according to instructions on page 76 and allow to dry thoroughly.

Using the photo as a guide, make a French knot for the nose and for each of the eyes with embroidery needle and floss (see page 77). Bury thread ends inside mouse head.

Stuff the mouse with fiberfill and put some catnip in last. Sew the mouse closed using the sewing needle and thread.

felted furry cat toys

hese furry cat toys are knit from wool yarn combined with eyelash yarn. The items are then thrown into the washing machine to felt them. If you have a kitten or a cat that eats string, make the plain versions instead.

SKILL LEVEL

Ball: Intermediate ■■■□

Tube: Beginner ■□□□

FINISHED MEASUREMENTS

Ball: Approx 4" diameter (after felting)

Tube: Approx 4 (6)" long (after felting)

Exact size is determined during felting.

MATERIALS

A 1 ball each of Galway Worsted from Plymouth Yarn (100% wool; 210 yds; 100 g) in desired color 4

B 1 ball each of Colorlash* from Plymouth Yarn (100% polyester; 220 yds; 201 m) in desired color 4

OR

1 ball each of Galway Chunky from Plymouth Yarn (100% wool; 123 yds; 100 g) in desired color 3

NOTE: One ball each of A and B will make several toys.

Tapestry needle

Stitch marker

> ***Warning:*** If you have kittens or cats that eat strings, do not make these toys with the eyelash yarn. Instead use a single strand of bulky-weight wool yarn. Cats can sustain serious intestinal injuries and even die from eating strings.

Ball

Set of 5 size 11 (8 mm) double-pointed needles or size to obtain gauge

2 large jingle bells

Size 7 (4.5mm) crochet hook (optional)

Tube

Size 11 (8 mm) straight needles or size to obtain gauge

Several 12"-long pieces of cotton yarn

Polyester fiberfill for stuffing

GAUGE

12 sts = 4" in St st using 1 strand each of A and B held tog or 1 strand of bulky weight (before felting)

Exact gauge is not critical. Make sure your stitches are open and airy for felting.

STOCKINETTE STITCH

Knit RS rows; purl WS rows.

BALL INSTRUCTIONS

With 1 strand each of A and B held tog (or 1 strand of bulky weight), CO 12 sts. Distribute evenly over 4 dpns—3 sts on each needle. Join to knit in the rnd, being careful not to twist sts. Pm to denote beg of rnd. Knit 1 rnd.

Rnd 1: *K1f&b, knit to last st on needle, K1f&b. Rep from * to end of rnd.

Rnd 2: Knit.

Rep rnds 1 and 2 until you have 13 sts on each needle—52 sts total.

Work even for 6 rnds.

Beg dec rnds:

Rnd 1: *K2tog, knit to last 2 sts on needle, K2tog, rep from * to end of rnd.

Rnd 2: Knit.

Rep rnds 1 and 2 until 3 sts rem on each needle—12 sts total.

Cut yarn, thread tail through rem sts, pull tight, and fasten off.

Finishing

Felt ball according to instructions on page 76 and allow to dry thoroughly.

Put 2 jingle bells into ball. Sew opening on ball closed.

If desired, make a 24"-long crochet chain and tie it onto the ball so you can swing it around to play with your cat.

TUBE INSTRUCTIONS

With 1 strand each of A and B held tog (or 1 strand of bulky weight), CO 25 (35) sts.

Work in St st for 2", ending after a WS row.

Eyelet row (RS): (K2tog, YO), rep to last st, K1.

Next row (WS): Purl.

Cont in St st until piece measures approx 6 (9)".

Rep eyelet row.

Work in St st for another 2", ending after a WS row.

BO all sts.

Finishing

Sew the long edges of the piece tog, forming a tube.

Weave one 12"-long piece of cotton yarn through the eyelets on each end of the toy. Tie the ends of the string tog.

Felt tube and allow to dry thoroughly.

Stuff with fiberfill. Cut ends of cotton yarn open. Pull ends of cotton yarn tight to close ends of toy and secure with a tight knot. Bury ends inside toy.

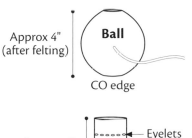

Approx 4" (after felting) — **Ball** — CO edge

Approx 4" (after felting) — **Tube** — Eyelets

felted **cat bed** with needle-felted mouse

Some kittens dream of hunting mice while they're sleeping, and this bed is for them! Made out of wool and felted, it's warm and cuddly. A needle-felted mouse in the center keeps kitty company.

SKILL LEVEL

Intermediate ◼◼◼◻

FINISHED MEASUREMENTS

Approx 15" in diameter x 4" high (after felting)

Exact size is determined during felting.

MATERIALS

Galway Worsted from Plymouth Yarn (100% wool; 210 yds; 100 g) (4)

A 2 balls of color 116 (blue)

B 2 balls of color 130 (green)

Size 13 (9 mm) circular needle (20" long) or size to obtain gauge

Size 13 (9 mm) double-pointed needles

10 stitch markers

Tapestry needle for weaving in ends

Heavy-duty felting needle, 38-gauge star point

Needle-felting mat

Tracing paper and Magic Marker (optional)

GAUGE

Approx 12 sts = 4" in St st with 2 strands of yarn held tog (before felting)

Exact gauge is not critical. Make sure your stitches are open and airy for felting.

STOCKINETTE STITCH (CIRCULAR)

Knit every st in every rnd.

INSTRUCTIONS

The sides of the bed are knit first, and then the bottom.

Sides

With 1 strand each of A and B held tog, CO 120 sts. Pm and join to knit in the rnd, being careful not to twist sts.

Work in St st for 2". Cut B and add a second strand of A. Work even until piece measures 6".

BO using a 4-st I-cord BO (see page 74).

Bottom

With 2 strands of B held tog and RS facing out, PU 120 sts on inside of bottom, along first purl row just inside I-cord BO edge.

Knit 1 rnd, pm after every 12th st—10 sections with 12 sts each.

Work dec as follows:

Rnd 1: (Knit to 2 sts before marker, K2tog) around.

Rnds 2 and 3: Knit.

Rep rnds 1–3 until 4 sts rem in each section, then work rnd 1 every other rnd until 2 sts rem in each section. Change to dpns when sts no longer fit on circular needle.

K2tog around.

Cut yarn, leaving a 6" tail. Run tail through rem sts and fasten off.

FINISHING

Felt according to instructions on page 76. Shape and press bottom of bed with a hot iron if necessary to make it flat. Allow bed to dry thoroughly.

Needle felt mouse on inside of bed bottom using A and the drawing below as a guide. If you are not comfortable doing this freehand, trace the drawing onto tracing paper. Make pinholes in the drawing; then hold the tracing over the bed bottom and transfer the outline onto the bed bottom with Magic Marker. Or, make a template of the mouse shape and trace around it with a marker. Be sure to cover all the marker lines with needle felting.

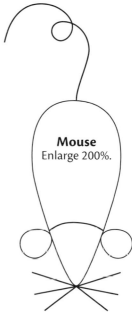

Mouse
Enlarge 200%.

felted kitty doorknob toy

This funny little toy hooks onto the doorknob to amuse your cat while you are away at work or out running errands. The pieces are knitted separately and sewn together. The toy is felted to give it body and so that kitty's nails won't get stuck in the stitches. The cat's extra-long and floppy legs end with bobble-shaped feet that dance in the air to keep your cat entertained.

SKILL LEVEL

Easy ■■☐☐

FINISHED MEASUREMENTS

Approx 4" wide x 16" long with 12" dangles (after felting)

Exact size is determined during felting.

MATERIALS

A 1 ball of Galway Worsted from Plymouth Yarn (100% wool; 210 yds; 100 g), color 117 (fuchsia) ④

B 1 ball of Furlauro from Plymouth Yarn (100% nylon; 82 yds; 50 g), color 816 (multi) ④

2 size 11 (8 mm) double-pointed needles or size to obtain gauge

Tapestry needle

1 yard of black embroidery floss

Sharp-pointed embroidery needle

GAUGE

Approx 12 sts = 4" in St st with 1 strand each of A and B held tog (before felting)

Exact gauge is not critical. Make sure your stitches are open and airy for felting.

INSTRUCTIONS

Make pieces separately and join them together before felting.

Body

With 1 strand each of A and B held tog, CO 10 sts.

Work 10 st I-cord for 12" (see page 74). Note that there will be a ladder of loose sts across back of I-cord. Don't worry about it; it will close up when felted.

BO all sts. Sew CO and BO edges tog to form a doughnut.

Legs (Make 4)

With 1 strand of A, CO 4 sts.

Work 4-st I-cord for 13".

Add 1 strand of B.

Next row: (K1, K1tbl, K1) in each st—12 sts. Do not turn. Slide sts to other end of dpn.

Work 12-st I-cord for 1" (paw).

Next row: K3tog 4 times—4 sts. Do not turn. Slide sts to other end of dpn.

Next row: K2tog twice, pass first st over second. Fasten off.

Tail

With 1 strand of A, CO 2 sts.

Work 2-st I-cord for 6".

BO all sts.

Head (Make 2 Pieces)

With 1 strand of A, CO 7 sts.

Knit 1 row, purl 1 row.

Next row (RS): K1, M1, knit to last st, M1, K1.

Next row: Purl.

Rep last 2 rows until you have 13 sts. End after working a WS row.

Knit 1 row, purl 1 row.

Next row (RS): K2tog, knit to last 2 sts, K2tog—11 sts rem.

Next row: Purl.

Next row (RS): K4, BO 3, K3—4 sts rem for each ear.

Ears

Next row (WS): P4.

Next row: K1, K2tog, K1.

Next row: P3.

Next row: K3tog.

Fasten off.

With WS facing, reattach yarn to second ear and rep the 4 rows of ear shaping.

FINISHING

With WS tog, sew 2 head pieces tog, placing pieces of wool yarn inside head for stuffing. Sew legs and tail to toy using photo as a guide. Weave in ends.

Felt according to instructions on page 76 and allow to dry. Embroider face, using French knots for eyes and nose (see page 77) and straight sts for whiskers. Sew head onto toy using photo as a guide. Bury ends inside of head.

scandinavian **pullover** for men and women

this sweater features a Scandinavian pattern that looks subtly like kittens. Combined with other traditional designs, this unisex sweater is knit in the round on circular needles so you never have to purl with two colors. Made in neutral colors, it's a design even a guy would wear. Made in brighter colors, it's fun for those who like a little extra flair.

SKILL LEVEL

Experienced ◼◼◼▬

FINISHED BUST/CHEST

37 (41½, 46, 50½, 55, 59½)"

MATERIALS

Country 8 Ply from Plymouth Yarn (100% superwash wool; 105 yds; 50 g) ④

Men's Sweater

A   6 (6, 8, 8, 10, 10) balls of color 2234 (cream)

B   4 (4, 6, 6, 8, 8) balls of color 2276 (moss green)

C   3 (3, 5, 5, 7, 7) balls of color 2256 (tan)

D   3 (3, 5, 5, 7, 7) balls of color 2266 (rust)

E   3 (3, 5, 5, 7, 7) balls of color 2271 (brown)

Women's Sweater

A   6 (6, 8, 8, 10, 10) balls of color 19 (cream)

B   4 (4, 6, 6, 8, 8) balls of color 2181 (navy blue)

C   3 (3, 5, 5, 7, 7) balls of color 2269 (gold)

D   3 (3, 5, 5, 7, 7) balls of color 2265 (green)

E   3 (3, 5, 5, 7, 7) balls of color 2160 (burgundy)

Size 7 (4.75mm) circular needles (29" and 16" long) or size to obtain gauge

Set of 4 or 5 size 7 (4.75) double-pointed needles

Size 5 (3.75mm) circular needles (29" and 16" long)

Set of 4 or 5 size 5 (3.75mm) double-pointed needles

Size 4 (3.5mm) circular needle (16" long) for neck facing

Stitch markers

Stitch holders (optional)

Tapestry needle

Extra needle for three-needle bind off

GAUGE

22 sts and 24 rows – 4" over charted patts

Always take time to check your gauge.

RIBBING (CIRCULAR)

Every rnd: (K2, P2) around.

STOCKINETTE STITCH (CIRCULAR)

Knit every st in every rnd.

REVERSE STOCKINETTE STITCH (CIRCULAR)

Purl every st in every rnd.

INSTRUCTIONS

The sweater is worked in the round from the bottom up.

Body

With 29" size 5 circular needle and A, CO 184 (208, 232, 256, 280, 304) sts. Pm and join to knit in the rnd, being careful not to twist sts. Work in K2, P2 ribbing for 2½" from CO edge.

Rib-to-Body Increase

Next rnd: Change to 29" size 7 circular needle and St st. Inc 20 sts evenly around—204 (228, 252, 276, 300, 324) sts.

Next rnd: Work 102 (114, 126, 138, 150, 162) sts, place a second marker. Work to end of rnd.

Body Stripe Pattern

Beg working charts in body stripe patt as follows:

Chart A, colors A and B

Chart B, colors B and C: dec 1 (inc 3, inc 0, dec 3, inc 1, dec 2) sts in last rnd of chart B—203 (231, 252, 273, 301, 322) sts.

Chart C, colors C and D: inc 1 (dec 3, dec 0, inc 3, dec 1, inc 2) sts in last rnd of chart C—204 (228, 252, 276, 300, 324) sts.

Chart D, colors D and E

Chart A, colors E and A

Chart B, colors A and B: dec 1 (inc 3, inc 0, dec 3, inc 1, dec 2) sts in last rnd of chart B—203 (231, 252, 273, 301, 322) sts.

Chart C, colors B and C: inc 1 (dec 3, dec 0, inc 3, dec 1, inc 2) sts in last rnd of chart C—204 (228, 252, 276, 300, 324) sts.

Chart D, colors C and D

Chart A, colors D and E

Cont in this fashion, inc or dec as indicated for your size in last rnd of charts B and C until piece measures 13½ (14, 15, 15, 15, 15)" or desired length to underarm. If this falls in chart C, work rem rows of chart C, inc or dec as specified in final rnd.

Armhole Steek Stitches

A steek is a set of extra sts that will later be cut to create neck and armhole openings.

Rnd 1: (Work to 3 sts before side marker, BO 6 sts) twice.

Rnd 2: (Work to bound-off sts, pm, CO 6 sts, pm) twice.

Work even in stripe patts, working steek sts in chart E and lining up other charts with arrangements on body until piece measures 19½ (21, 23, 24, 25, 25½)". If this falls in chart C, work rem rows of chart C, inc or dec as required for your size in final rnd.

Neck Shaping

Rnd 1: From first marker, work 36 (42, 46, 52, 56, 62) sts in patt. BO center 24 (24, 28, 28, 32, 32) sts. Work in patt to side marker, sm. Work back sts in patt.

Rnd 2: Work to bound-off sts, pm, CO 6 steek sts, pm. Complete rnd.

Rnd 3: Work to 4 sts before first steek marker, K2tog, K2, work steek sts in chart E, sm, K2, ssk, complete rnd in patt.

Rnd 4: Work even in patts as est.

Rep rnds 3 and 4 another 5 (5, 6, 6, 7, 7) times—24 (30, 32, 38, 40, 46) sts rem for each shoulder.

Work even in stripe patts as est and work steek sts in chart E until piece measures 22½ (24, 26, 27, 28, 28½)".

BO all sts or put shoulder sts on holders.

Sleeves

With size 5 dpns and A, CO 52 (52, 56, 56, 60, 60) sts. Divide sts on 3 or 4 dpns. Join to knit in the rnd, being careful not to twist sts. Pm to denote beg of rnd.

Work K2, P2 ribbing until cuff measures 2½" from CO edge.

Cuff-to-Sleeve-Increase Round

Change to size 7 dpns and St st, inc 2 (2, 4, 4, 0, 0) sts evenly around—54 (54, 60, 60, 60, 60) sts.

Sleeve Shaping

Beg working charts in stripe patt following same color sequence as on body, and AT SAME TIME inc 1 st on each side of marker every second rnd 4 times, then every fourth rnd 19 (24, 27, 32, 38, 40) times—100 (110, 122, 132, 144, 148) sts. Work incs into patts, changing to 16" size 7 circular needle when sts no longer fit on dpns. Work even in stripe patt until piece measures 19 (20, 21, 22, 22, 22)". Cont in last color worked and rev St st, work even for ½" for armhole facing.

BO all sts.

FINISHING

With sewing machine or hand stitching, baste up the center of the 6 steek sts at each armhole and at the neck. Sew 2 rows of machine or hand stitching 1 st to right and left of basting and across bottom. Remove basting and cut down the center with sharp sewing shears.

Sew shoulder seams.

With RS facing, insert sleeve into armhole and sew last rnd of St st on sleeves to armhole, easing to fit. Turn sweater inside out, and sew down armhole facing, covering cut edge at armhole.

Rep for second sleeve.

Neckband

With RS facing you, 16" size 5 circular needle, and A, PU 94 (94, 104, 104, 114, 114) sts around neck edge. Knit 1 rnd.

For men's: Work in K1, P1 ribbing for 1¼" or desired length. Change to size 4 needle. Knit 1 rnd. Work in K1, P1 ribbing for 1½" or desired length.

For women's: Work in K2, P2 ribbing for 1¼" or desired length. Change to size 4 needle and work in St st for 1½" or desired length.

BO all sts loosely in patt.

Fold neckband to inside and sew down, covering cut edge at front neck.

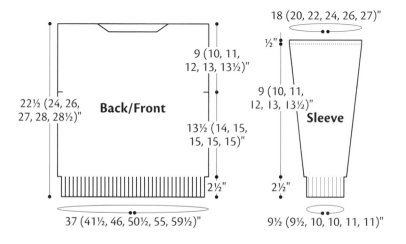

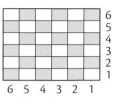

18 (20, 22, 24, 26, 27)"

9 (10, 11, 12, 13, 13½)"

Back/Front

Sleeve

22½ (24, 26, 27, 28, 28½)"

13½ (14, 15, 15, 15, 15)"

9 (10, 11, 12, 13, 13½)"

2½"

2½"

37 (41½, 46, 50½, 55, 59½)"

9½ (9½, 10, 10, 11, 11)"

Chart A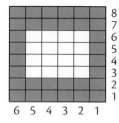
8 7 6 5 4 3 2 1
6 5 4 3 2 1

Chart B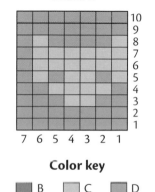
11 10 9 8 7 6 5 4 3 2 1
6 5 4 3 2 1

Chart C
10 9 8 7 6 5 4 3 2 1
7 6 5 4 3 2 1

Chart D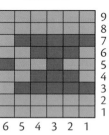
9 8 7 6 5 4 3 2 1
6 5 4 3 2 1

Chart E
6 5 4 3 2 1
6 5 4 3 2 1

Use colors as established when working chart E.

Color key

 A   B   C   D   E

ballet **cardigan**

a stylized cat design decorates the front of this wrap cardigan for advanced knitters. Made with two shades of the same-color yarn, the design is understated and elegant. Lace stitches add a touch of class, and attached I-cord trim finishes it off perfectly.

SKILL LEVEL

Experienced ◼◼◼◻

FINISHED MEASUREMENTS

Bust: Approx 34 (40, 46, 52)" when wrapped

Back Neck to Waist Length: 17 (19, 21, 22)"

MATERIALS

Country Silk 8 Ply from Plymouth Yarn (85% wool, 15% silk; 105 yds; 50 g) ④

MC 7 (9, 11, 13) balls of color 2 (pink)

CC 1 (1, 2, 2) balls of color 7 (fuchsia)

Size 6 (4 mm) circular needle (at least 24" long) or size to obtain gauge

2 size 6 (4 mm) double-pointed needles

Stitch markers

Stitch holders

Tapestry needle

Small snaps (optional)

Sewing needle and matching thread (optional)

GAUGE

22 sts and 24 rows = 4" in St st

STOCKINETTE STITCH

Knit RS rows; purl WS rows.

RIBBING

Worked over an even number of sts

Every row: (K1, P1) across.

EYELET LACE PATTERN

See chart on page 32.

INSTRUCTIONS

When inc and dec in lace patt, if you do not have enough sts to work a full motif, work extra sts in St st.

Work back first so you are familiar with eyelet lace patt before you beg left front, which requires more complex shaping to be worked around patt.

Back

With MC and circular needle, CO 80 (96, 112, 128) sts.

Work 4 rows in eyelet lace patt.

WAIST SHAPING

Inc row (RS): Maintaining eyelet lace patt, inc 1 st at beg and end of row—82 (98, 114, 130) sts.

Work 3 rows even.

Rep these 4 rows another 4 times, then work inc row once more—92 (108, 124, 140) sts.

Work even in lace patt until piece measures 9 (10, 11, 12)" from beg. End after working a WS row.

ARMHOLE SHAPING

Maintaining patt, BO 4 sts at beg of next 2 rows, then BO 3 sts at beg of next 2 rows—78 (94, 110, 126) sts.

Next 2 (3, 3, 4) RS rows: K2, ssk, work in eyelet lace patt as est to last 4 sts, K2tog, K2—74 (88, 104, 118) sts rem.

Work even in lace patt until piece measures 16 (18, 20, 22)" from beg, ending after working a WS row.

SHOULDER SHAPING

BO 6 (7, 9, 11) sts at beg of next 6 rows.

Put rem 38 (46, 50, 52) sts on holder for back neck.

Right Front

With MC, CO 75 (87, 99, 114) sts; with CC, CO 3 sts—78 (90, 102, 117) sts.

Beg working St st with I-cord edging as follows:

Row 1 and 3 (RS): With CC, K3 loosely so I-cord does not draw in, change to MC, twisting the colors using intarsia technique (see page 75), P2, knit to end of row.

Row 2 and 4 (WS): With MC, purl to last 5 sts, K2, slip last 3 sts to RH needle.

Cont in patts as est and AT SAME TIME beg waist shaping at side edge and beg wrap shaping at front edge as follows:

WAIST SHAPING AT SIDE EDGE

Inc row (RS): Inc 1 st at end of row.

Work 3 rows even.

Rep these 4 rows another 4 times, then work inc row once more (total of 5 sts inc at side edge).

WRAP SHAPING AT FRONT EDGE

AT SAME TIME, work wrap shaping as follows:

Row 1, dec row (RS): With CC, K3, change to MC, P2, ssk, knit to end of row.

Row 2 (WS): Work in patts as est.

Rep rows 1 and 2 for wrap shaping until piece measures approx 9 (10, 11, 12)" from beg, end after working a WS row.

Cont working wrap shaping in patts as est and AT SAME TIME beg armhole shaping as follows:

BO 4 sts at beg of next WS row, then BO 3 sts at beg of next WS row.

Next 2 (3, 3, 4) WS rows: P2, P2tog, work in patts to end of row.

Cont wrap shaping until 23 (26, 32, 38) sts rem at shoulder, including edge and I-cord sts.

Work even until piece measures 16 (18, 20, 22)" from beg, end after working a WS row.

SHOULDER SHAPING

BO 6 (7, 9, 11) sts at beg of next 3 WS rows.

BO rem 2 purl sts.

Put 3 I-cord edging sts on holder.

Left Front

With CC and circular needle, CO 3 sts; with MC, CO 75 (87, 99, 114) sts—78 (90, 102, 117) sts.

Beg working eyelet lace patt with I-cord edging as follows:

Row 1 (RS): With MC, work lace patt row 1 (knit across) to last 6 (10, 6, 5) sts, K1 (5, 1, 0), P2, yarn to back, sl last 3 sts to RH needle.

Row 2 and all even rows (WS): With CC, P3 loosely so I-cord does not draw in; change to MC, twisting colors using intarsia technique (see page 74), K2, work lace patt (purl across) to end of row.

NOTE: As the front edge of the piece becomes narrower with shaping, whenever you do not have enough stitches to complete a full repeat of the lace pattern before the last 5 sts, work the odd stitches in St st.

Row 3: With MC, work lace patt row 3 to last 6 (10, 6, 5) sts, K1 (5, 1, 0), P2, yarn to back, sl last 3 sts to RH needle.

Maintain patts as est and AT SAME TIME beg waist shaping at side edge and beg wrap shaping at front edge as described below.

WAIST SHAPING AT SIDE EDGE

Inc row (RS): Inc 1 st at beg of row.

Work 3 rows even.

Rep these 4 rows another 4 times, then work inc row once more (total of 6 sts inc).

Remember to work inc in St st and then into lace patt when you have enough sts for a full motif.

WRAP SHAPING AT FRONT EDGE

AT SAME TIME, work wrap shaping as follows:

Row 1, dec row (RS): With MC, work in patt to last 7 sts, K2tog, P2, yarn to back, sl last 3 sts to RH needle.

Row 2 (WS): Work in patts as est.

Rep rows 1 and 2 for wrap shaping until piece measures approx 9 (10, 11, 12)" from beg, ending after a WS row.

Cont working wrap shaping in patts as est and AT SAME TIME beg armhole shaping as follows:

BO 4 sts at beg of next RS row, then BO 3 sts at beg of next RS row.

Next 2 (3, 3, 4) RS rows: K2, ssk, work in patts to end of row.

Cont wrap shaping until 23 (26, 32, 38) sts rem at shoulder, including edge and I-cord sts.

Work even until piece measures 16 (18, 20, 22) from beg, ending after a WS row.

SHOULDER SHAPING

BO 6 (7, 9, 11) sts at beg of next 3 RS rows.

BO rem 2 purl sts.

Put 3 I-cord edging sts on holder.

Sleeves

Make 2, with differences for right and left sleeve as noted.

With CC, CO 48 (56, 64, 72) sts.

Work in K1, P1 ribbing for ½". Change to MC.

Right sleeve: Beg working in St st.

Left sleeve: Beg working in eyelet lace patt.

Both sleeves, inc row (RS): Inc 1 st at beg and end of row—50 (58, 66, 74) sts.

Work 3 rows even.

Cont to inc at beg and end of every 4 rows until you have 66 (78, 88, 100) sts.

Work even until piece measures 12 (12, 13, 13)" from beg, ending after a WS row.

CAP SHAPING

BO 4 sts at beg of next 2 rows, then BO 3 sts at beg of next 2 rows.

Next 4 (6, 6, 8) RS rows: K2, ssk, knit to last 4 sts, K2tog, K2. End after a WS row.

BO 3 sts at beg of next 2 rows, then BO 4 sts at beg of next 4 rows.

Place rem 22 (30, 40, 48) sts on holder.

FINISHING

Sew shoulder seams.

Referring to chart on page 33 and photo on page 28, work a duplicate-st cat motif on the right front, placing the cat approx 15 rows from the bottom and 15 sts from the side edge.

With RS facing you, put back neck sts on needle. Then put right-front I-cord sts on tip of same needle. Work I-cord BO across all back neck sts (see page 74). Graft 3 sts rem on needle to 3 sts from left front I-cord edging.

Sew sleeves into armholes. Sew underarm seams and sew fronts to back at sides.

With RS facing you, circular needle, and MC, PU 1 st in each CO st along bottom edge of sweater body. Set aside. Using CC and dpns, CO 3 sts. Work I-cord for 12 (14, 16, 18)". Hold the sweater with RS facing you and upside down, so the waist is at the top. Slip 3 sts from dpn onto circular needle at right edge of piece. Work I-cord BO across all picked-up sts at bottom of sweater across to left edge of piece. Put rem 3 sts on dpn. Work I-cord for 12 (14, 16, 18)". BO all sts. Make 2 more pieces of I-cord 12 (14, 16, 18)" long. Sew an I-cord to the inside of each side seam.

To wear, tie sweater closed at sides. If desired, sew snaps on fronts at neck for a more modest fit.

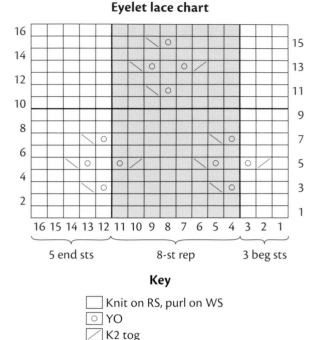

Eyelet lace chart

Key

Knit on RS, purl on WS
YO
K2 tog
Ssk
Shaded area is pattern repeat

5 end sts   8-st rep   3 beg sts

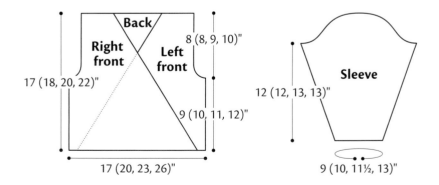

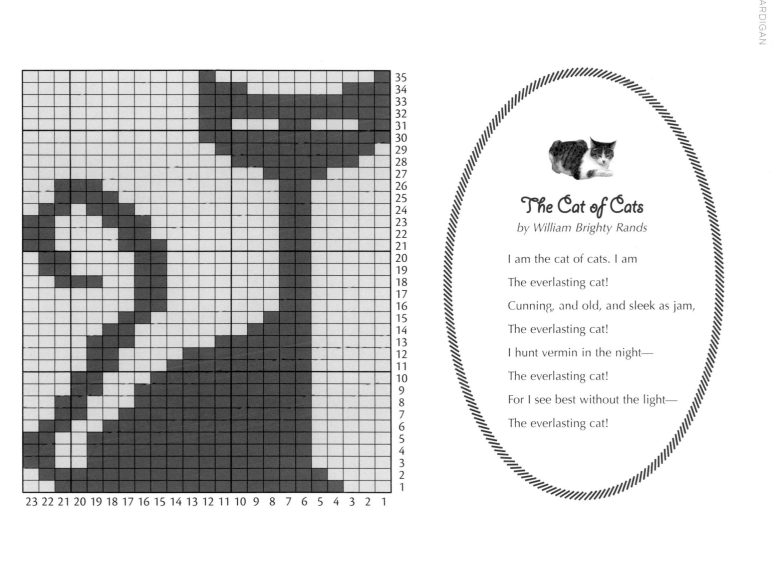

23 22 21 20 19 18 17 16 15 14 13 12 11 10 9 8 7 6 5 4 3 2 1

The Cat of Cats

by William Brighty Rands

I am the cat of cats. I am

The everlasting cat!

Cunning, and old, and sleek as jam,

The everlasting cat!

I hunt vermin in the night—

The everlasting cat!

For I see best without the light—

The everlasting cat!

felted kitty slippers shaped with short rows will keep your toes toasty even on the coldest winter nights. When you're in the mood to share the evening with your cats, put on these slippers, snuggle up on the couch, and pop your favorite movie into the DVD player.

SKILL LEVEL

Experienced ■■■▶

FINISHED MEASUREMENTS

Approx 9 (10, 11)" long (after felting)

Exact size is determined during felting.

MATERIALS

A 2 (2, 3) balls of Galway Worsted from Plymouth Yarn (100% wool; 210 yds; 100 g), color 139 (dark aqua) **4**

B 4 (5, 5) balls of Firenze from Plymouth Yarn (30% wool, 30% acrylic, 40% nylon; 55 yds; 50 g), color 431 (blue/green multi) **4**

Size 15 (10 mm) circular needle (16" long) or size to obtain gauge

2 size 15 (10 mm) double-pointed needles

Size 7 (4.5 mm) needles

Safety pin

Stitch markers

Tapestry needle

2 squares of felt, 1 black and 1 turquoise

Washable craft glue

Shiny or metallic embroidery thread

Embroidery needle

GAUGE

Approx 11 sts = 4" in garter st with 2 strands of A held tog on larger needles (before felting)

Exact gauge is not critical. Make sure your stitches are open and airy for felting.

GARTER STITCH

Knit every st in every row.

(Two rows of garter st equals 1 ridge.)

INSTRUCTIONS

Make 2 slippers alike.

Sole

Using 2 strands of A held tog and larger needles, CO 5 sts.

Inc row: K1, K1f&b, knit to end of row.

Rep inc row until you have 11 (13, 15) sts.

Knit every row with no inc until you have 26 (28, 30) garter ridges—52 (56, 60) rows from beg.

Dec row: K1, K2tog, knit to end of row.

Rep dec row until 5 sts rem.

BO all sts.

Front of Slipper (Cat Head)

Choose a side as RS and mark it with a safety pin. With RS facing you, count back 17 (18, 19) ridges from the 5 CO sts.

Starting at 17th (18th, 19th) ridge, with 1 strand of A and larger needles, PU 17 (18, 19) sts along side of foot, pm, PU 5 sts along CO edge, pm, PU 17 (18, 19) sts along other side of foot—39 (41, 43) sts.

Add 1 strand of B, and holding both yarns tog, work in short rows as follows:

Setup row (WS): K17 (18, 19), sm, K5, sm, K17 (18, 19). Turn.

Row 1 (RS): K17 (18, 19), sm, K5, sm, K2. Turn.

Row 2 (WS): K2, sm, K5, sm, K2. Turn.

Row 3: K2, sm, K5, sm, K3. Turn.

Row 4: K3, sm, K5, sm, K3. Turn.

Row 5: K3, sm, K1f&b, K3, K1f&b, sm, K4. Turn. (7 sts between markers)

Row 6: K4, sm, K7, sm, K4. Turn.

Row 7: K4, sm, K7, sm, K5. Turn.

Row 8: K5, sm, K7, sm, K5. Turn.

Row 9: K5, sm, K1f&b, K5, K1f&b, sm, K6. Turn. (9 sts between markers)

Row 10: K6, sm, K9, sm, K6. Turn.

Row 11: K6, sm, K9, sm, K7. Turn.

Row 12: K7, sm, K9, sm, K8, Turn.

Row 13: K7, sm, K1f&b, K7, K1f&b, sm, K8. Turn. (11 sts between markers)

Row 14: K8, sm, K11, sm, K8. Turn.

Row 15: K8, sm, K11, sm, K9. Turn.

Row 16: K9, sm, K11, sm, K9. Turn

Rep rows 15 and 16 with no additional inc between markers, working 1 additional st at end of each row until 1 st rem unworked at each end of row.

Next row (RS): K1, K2tog, knit to first marker, sm, K2tog, knit to 2 sts before second marker, K2tog, sm, knit to last 3 sts, K2tog, K1. Turn.

Next row (WS): Knit all sts. Turn.

BO all sts.

Use tails to fasten ends of front securely to sole.

Heel

Starting in same st as front of foot with RS facing you, using 1 strand of A and larger needles, PU 11 (13, 15) sts along side of heel, PU 5 sts along BO edge, PU 11 (13, 15) sts along other side of heel—27 (31, 35) sts.

Add 1 strand of B and holding both yarns tog, knit 12 rows.

Dec row: K2, K2tog, K6, K2tog, knit to last 12 sts, K2tog, K6, K2tog, K2.

BO all sts.

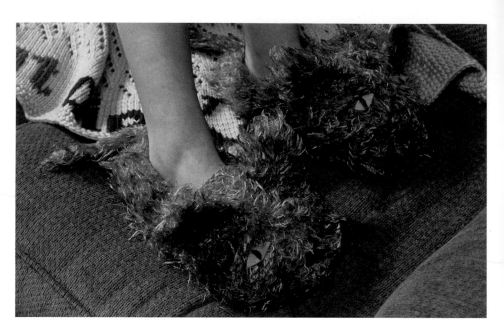

Tail

With 1 strand each of A and B held tog and dpns, CO 4 sts. Work I-cord (see page 74) for 5".

BO all sts. Sew tail to center of heel.

Ears (Make 2)

With 1 strand each of A and B held tog and larger needles, CO 10 sts. Knit 2 rows.

Dec row: K2tog, knit to end of row.

Rep dec row until 2 sts rem. K2tog. Fasten off.

Sew ears onto head 3 ridges from BO edge and approx 1" apart.

FINISHING

Sew front to heel at side seams. Weave in ends.

Felt according to instructions on page 76.

If desired, trim ears. Cut out eyes, pupils, and nose from felt using photo or your imagination as a guide. Glue face pieces to slipper.

Cut embroidery thread into eight 6" lengths and sew 4 pieces to each side of face for whiskers. Trim even if desired.

Strap

With smaller needles and 1 strand of A, CO 20 sts. Knit 4 rows. BO all sts loosely.

Sew strap to instep, just behind head, to pull slipper tog and make it fit snugly. This will also help shape the face.

Three Little Kittens
by Mother Goose

Three little kittens,
They lost their mittens,
And they began to cry,
Oh, mother dear,
We sadly fear
Our mittens we have lost.

What! Lost your mittens,
You naughty kittens!
Then you shall have no pie.
Mee-ow, mee-ow, mee-ow.
No, you shall have no pie.

The three little kittens,
They found their mittens,
And they began to cry,
Oh, mother dear,
See here, see here,
Our mittens we have found.

What! Found your mittens,
You silly kittens!
Then you shall have some pie.
Purr-r, purr-r, purr-r,
Oh, let us have some pie.

The three little kittens,
Put on their mittens,
And soon ate up the pie;
Oh, mother dear,
We greatly fear
Our mittens we have soiled.

What! Soiled your mittens,
You naughty kittens!
Then they began to sigh,
Mee-ow, mee-ow, mee-ow.
Then they began to sigh.

The three little kittens,
They washed their mittens,
And hung them out to dry;
Oh mother dear,
Look here, look here,
Our mittens we have washed.

What! Washed your mittens,
You're good little kittens.
But I smell a rat close by!
Hush! Hush! Hush!
I smell a rat close by.

color-work chullo

inspired by Marcia Lewandowski's *Andean Folk Knits*, this winter hat is perfect for a trip to the ski slopes or the shopping mall. The ear flaps are knit flat; then the body of the hat is knit in the round on circular and double-pointed needles. Because the hat is knit with two colors in the Fair-Isle technique, it is windproof—using two colors creates yarn floats on the inside of the hat that add thickness.

SKILL LEVEL

Intermediate ◼◼◼◻

FINISHED MEASUREMENTS

20 (22)" circumference

MATERIALS

Galway Worsted from Plymouth Yarn
(100% wool; 210 yds; 100 g) 〖4〗

A 1 skein of color 91 (orange)

B 1 skein of color 147 (yellow)

C 1 skein of color 8 (white)

D 1 skein of color 127 (green)

E 1 skein of color 134 (gray)

Size 5 (6) [3.75 (4) mm] circular
needle (16" long) or size to obtain
gauge

Set of 4 or 5 size 5 (6) [3.75 (4) mm]
double-pointed needles

Stitch markers

Size G-6 (4 mm) crochet hook

Tapestry needle for weaving in ends

GAUGE

6 (5½) sts = 4" in chart patt

INSTRUCTIONS

Both sizes are worked the same. The
difference in gauge and needle sizes
makes the smaller and larger sizes.
Use the needle size required to get the
correct gauge for the desired size. Use
the Fair-Isle technique on page 74.

Ear Flaps (Make 2)

Using C and dpns, CO 3 sts.

Row 1 (RS): Knit.

Rows 2 and 4 (WS): Purl.

Row 3: K1, M1, K1, M1, K1—5 sts.

Row 5: K1, M1, knit to last st, M1,
K1—7 sts.

Row 6: Purl.

Rep rows 5 and 6 until you have 21
sts.

Do not bind off. Set ear flaps aside.

Hat Body

Using circular needle and A, CO 17
sts, knit across 1 ear flap, CO 44 sts
(front of hat), knit across second ear
flap, CO 17 sts (center back of hat)—
120 sts. Pm, join to knit in the rnd.

Work all rnds of chart, changing
colors as indicated.

Knit 1 rnd with A.

Crown

Change to C and knit 1 rnd. Work
crown dec as follows, switching to
dpns when necessary:

Rnd 1: (K10, K2tog, pm) around—110
sts rem.

Rnd 2: Knit.

Rnd 3: (Knit to 2 sts before marker,
K2tog) around.

Rep rnds 2 and 3 until 20 sts rem.

K2tog around—10 sts rem.

Cut yarn, leaving a 6" tail. Thread tail
through rem sts and pull tight to fasten
off.

FINISHING

Using crochet hook and D, work 1 rnd
of sc around bottom edge of hat. Rep
with B and then with A. Fasten off.

Weave in ends.

Tassels

With D, make a crochet chain (see
page 77) approx 6" long. Work 1 row
of sc. Fasten off. Sew crochet strand
to center bottom of ear flap on inside
of flap.

With 1 strand each of A and B, make
a small tassel (see page 78) and attach
to bottom of crochet strand. Weave in
rem ends.

Rep for other side of hat

39

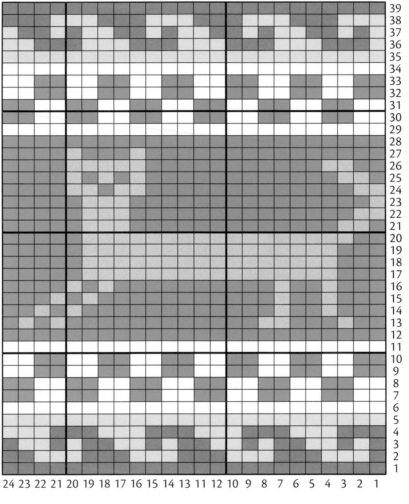

39
38
37
36
35
34
33
32
31
30
29
28
27
26
25
24
23
22
21
20
19
18
17
16
15
14
13
12
11
10
9
8
7
6
5
4
3
2
1

24 23 22 21 20 19 18 17 16 15 14 13 11 12 10 9 8 7 6 5 4 3 2 1

Color key

A (orange) D (green)
B (yellow) E (gray)
C (white)

The Owl and the Pussycat

by Edward Lear

I

The Owl and the Pussy-cat went to sea
In a beautiful pea green boat,
They took some honey, and plenty of money,
Wrapped up in a five pound note.
The Owl looked up to the stars above,
And sang to a small guitar,
'O lovely Pussy! O Pussy my love,
What a beautiful Pussy you are,
You are,
You are!
What a beautiful Pussy you are!'

II

Pussy said to the Owl, 'You elegant fowl!
How charmingly sweet you sing!
O let us be married! too long we have tarried:
But what shall we do for a ring?'
They sailed away, for a year and a day,
To the land where the Bong-tree grows

And there in a wood a Piggy-wig stood
With a ring at the end of his nose,
His nose,
His nose,
With a ring at the end of his nose.

III

'Dear pig, are you willing to sell for one shilling
Your ring?' Said the Piggy, 'I will.'
So they took it away, and were married next day
By the Turkey who lives on the hill.
They dined on mince, and slices of quince,
Which they ate with a runcible spoon;
And hand in hand, on the edge of the sand,
They danced by the light of the moon,
The moon,
The moon,
They danced by the light of the moon.

cat-ears **hat**

this beginner winter hat can be made in an evening using plain garter stitch (no purls!), so it's a perfect last-minute gift for the cat lover on your list. The funky design is perfect for teens—or grannies who have a whimsical side.

SKILL LEVEL

Beginner ■□□□

FINISHED MEASUREMENTS

17" circumference*

*This hat is very stretchy and fits most adult heads easily.

MATERIALS

2 balls of Encore Chunky Colorspun from Plymouth Yarn (75% acrylic, 25% wool; 143 yds; 100 g), color 7128 (multi) 🔵3️⃣

Size 10 (6 mm) needles or size to obtain gauge

Size 8 (5 mm) needles

Tapestry needle

GAUGE

11 sts = 4" in garter st using larger needles

GARTER STITCH

Knit every st in every row.

INSTRUCTIONS

With smaller needles, CO 50 sts. Knit every row until piece measures 1½".

Change to larger needles. Cont working in garter st until piece measures 13".

BO all sts.

FINISHING

With RS facing up, and using mattress st, sew side seam, sew top seam.

Place hat on a flat surface with seam at one side. Sew diagonally across each ear to hold it in place.

Weave in ends and fold up brim.

Cut six 16" lengths of yarn. Fold 3 strands in half and pull one end through a st at bottom of brim on one side of hat. Braid the 6 strands tog.

Secure with a knot 1" from bottom of braid. Trim loose ends if desired. Rep on other side of hat.

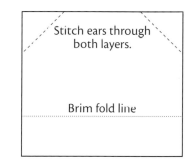

Stitch ears through both layers.

Brim fold line

43

i found this lacy adaptation of a Peruvian cat motif in a 1960s book by Dorothy Reade. She converted designs from many different kinds of textiles and artifacts into knitting designs. This lazy, lacy cat wants to cuddle around your neck and keep you warm while you run errands on a breezy afternoon or sit at your desk in a chilly office.

SKILL LEVEL

Intermediate ◼◼◼◻

FINISHED MEASUREMENTS

56" long x 7½" wide

MATERIALS

2 balls of Alpaca Sport 3 Ply from Plymouth Yarn (100% Peruvian alpaca; 185 yds; 50 g), color 100 (cream)

Size 6 (4 mm) needles or size to obtain gauge

Stitch holder or spare needle

Tapestry needle

GAUGE

20 sts = 4" in cat's paw lace patt, blocked

INSTRUCTIONS

This scarf is made in two pieces, worked from the end toward the center, with differences as noted. After the knitting is complete, the pieces are joined with kitchener stitch.

CO 10 sts.

Setup row (WS): Sl 1, purl to last st, K1.

NOTE: This scarf has a slip-st selvage. Slip the first st of each row as if to purl wyif.

Setup Border

Row 1 (RS): Sl 1, (P1, K1) twice, pm, M1, pm, (K1, P1) twice, K1.

Row 2 (WS): Sl 1, (P1, K1) twice, sm, purl to next marker, sm, (K1, P1) twice, K1.

Row 3: Sl 1, (P1, K1) twice, sm, M1, knit to next marker, M1, sm (K1, P1) twice, K1.

Rep rows 2 and 3 until you have 9 sts between markers—19 sts total.

Rep row 2 once more.

Beginning Cat Motif

Cont with border patt as est, working rows 1–48 of chart A between markers as follows:

Row 1 and all odd rows (RS): Sl 1, (P1, K1) twice, sm, work chart A sts to next marker, sm, (K1, P1) twice, K1.

Row 2 and all even rows (WS): Sl 1, (P1, K1) twice, sm, purl to next marker, sm, (K1, P1) twice, K1.

After completing row 48 of chart A, 30 sts rem between markers—40 sts total.

Cat's Paw Lace Pattern

Cont with border patt as est, work rows 1–20 of chart B between markers as follows:

Row 1 and all odd rows (RS): Sl 1, (P1, K1) twice, sm, work chart B sts to next marker, sm, (K1, P1) twice, K1.

Row 2 and all even rows (WS): Sl 1, (P1, K1) twice, sm, purl to next marker, sm, (K1, P1) twice, K1.

Rep all rows of chart B 6 times. Piece should measure approx 24" long.

First half only: Work rows 1–17 of chart B once more. Put sts on stitch holder or spare needle.

Second half only: Work rows 1–8 of chart B once more.

FINISHING

Join ends of scarf with kitchener st (see page 54). Weave in ends. Block to measurements (see page 76). Make 2 small tassels (see page 78). Attach a tassel to each end of the scarf, slightly gathering the ends of the scarf to form a point.

Chart A

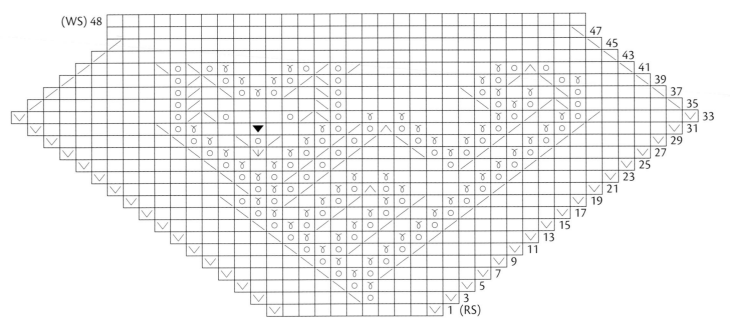

Stitch key

☐ Knit on RS, purl on WS	⊻ Knit into front and back of same stitch
ϒ K1 tbl	⋀ Sl 1 knitwise, K2tog, psso (double dec)
○ YO	⋁ M1
╱ K2tog (right slanting dec)	▼ Knit this st through open space below
╲ K2tog tbl (left slanting dec)	

Purl all WS (even) rows.

Chart B

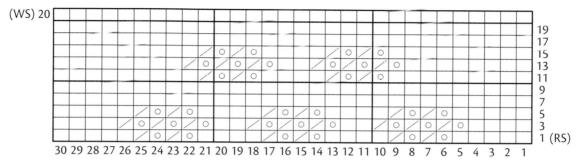

(WS) 20

19
17
15
13
11
9
7
5
3
1 (RS)

30 29 28 27 26 25 24 23 22 21 20 19 18 17 16 15 14 13 12 11 10 9 8 7 6 5 4 3 2 1

Stitch key

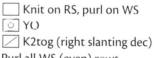

☐ Knit on RS, purl on WS

☐ YO

☐ K2tog (right slanting dec)

Purl all WS (even) rows.

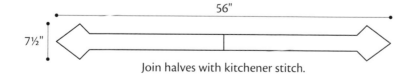

56"

7½"

Join halves with kitchener stitch.

hidden cat scarf

in illusion knitting, pictures are hidden between rows of plain knitting. The cats on this scarf show up if you look at just the right angle, but turn your head to one side or the other and they'll disappear between the stripes.

SKILL LEVEL

Easy ◖■◻◻

FINISHED MEASUREMENTS

74" long x 8½" wide (after blocking)

MATERIALS

Suri Merino from Plymouth Yarn (55% Suri alpaca, 45% extra fine merino; 109 yds; 50 g) (4)

A   3 balls of color 2037 (orange)

B   3 balls of color 402 (gray)

Size 7 (4.5 mm) needles or size to obtain gauge

Tapestry needle

GAUGE

20 sts = 4" in hidden cat patt

INSTRUCTIONS

With B, CO 40 sts.

Work chart 6 times, changing colors as indicated.

Cut A. With B, knit 2 rows.

BO with B.

FINISHING

Weave in ends.

Triangle Edging

With A and RS facing you, pick up 40 sts. Knit 1 row.

Rows 1 and 2: K2. Turn.

Rows 3 and 4: K3. Turn.

Rows 5 and 6: K4. Turn.

Rows 7 and 8: K5. Turn.

Rows 9 and 10: K6. Turn.

Rows 11 and 12: K7. Turn.

Rows 13 and 14: K8. Turn.

Rows 15 and 16: K9. Turn.

Rows 17 and 18: K10. Turn.

Row 19: BO 10 sts. To beg next triangle, K1—2 sts on RH needle.

Rep rows 2–19 another 3 times; do not K1 at end of last triangle. Fasten off.

With B and WS facing you, skip 5 sts, pick up 35 sts. Knit 1 row. Work 3 triangles as for orange section. Fasten off.

Rep both sets of triangles on other end of scarf, reversing colors.

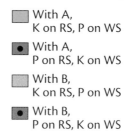

Color and stitch key

▢	With A, K on RS, P on WS
⬛●	With A, P on RS, K on WS
▢	With B, K on RS, P on WS
●	With B, P on RS, K on WS

The Kitten and the Falling Leaves

by William Wordsworth

That way look, my infant, lo!
What a pretty baby-show!
See the kitten on the wall,
sporting with the leaves that fall.
Withered leaves—one—two and three
from the lofty elder tree.
Through the calm and frosty air,
of this morning bright and fair.
Eddying round and round they sink,
softly, slowly; one might think.
From the motions that are made,
every little leaf conveyed
Sylph or Faery hither tending,
to this lower world descending.
Each invisible and mute,
in his wavering parachute.

But the Kitten, how she starts,
crouches, stretches, paws, and darts!
First at one, and then its fellow,
just as light and just as yellow.

There are many now—now one,
now they stop and there are none:
What intenseness of desire,
in her upward eye of fire!
With a tiger-leap half-way,
now she meets the coming prey.
lets it go as fast, and then;
Has it in her power again.
Now she works with three or four,
like an Indian conjuror;
quick as he in feats of art,
far beyond in joy of heart.
Where her antics played in the eye,
of a thousand standers-by,
clapping hands with shout and stare,
what would little Tabby care!
For the plaudits of the crowd?
Over happy to be proud,
over wealthy in the treasure
of her exceeding pleasure!

kitty socks

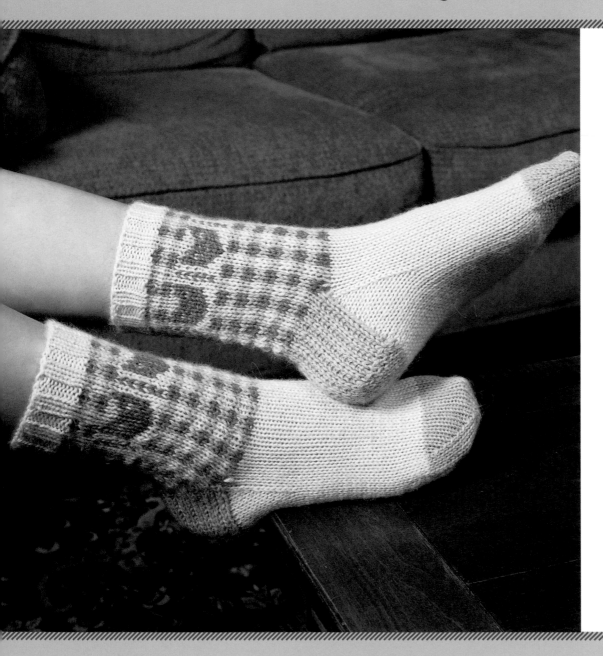

a row of kitty-cat heads encircles your ankles between sections of knitted gingham checks. These alpaca socks are warm enough for outdoor wear, but better for pampering your toes while reading in bed.

SKILL LEVEL

Intermediate ●■■□

SIZES

Women's Small (Medium, Large)

Finished Foot Circumference: 7½ (8, 8½)"

MATERIALS

Baby Alpaca DK from Plymouth Yarn (100% superfine baby alpaca; 125 yds; 50 g) ④

A 2 balls of color 100 (white)

B 1 ball of color 208 (tan)

C 1 ball of color 207 (beige)

Stitch marker

Stitch holder or spare needle

Tapestry needle

Small and Large Sizes

Set of 4 or 5 size 4 (3.5 mm) double-pointed needles or size to obtain gauge

Set of 4 or 5 size 3 (3.25 mm) double-pointed needles

Medium Size

Set of 4 or 5 size 3 (3.25 mm) double-pointed needles or size to obtain gauge

Set of 4 or 5 size 2 (2.75 mm) double-pointed needles

GAUGE

24 (26, 24) sts = 4" in St st on larger needles

RIBBING (CIRCULAR)

Every rnd: (K2, P2) around.

STOCKINETTE STITCH (CIRCULAR)

Knit every st in every rnd.

INSTRUCTIONS

Make 2 socks alike.

Leg

With smaller needles and A, CO 44 (52, 52) sts. Divide sts evenly on 3 or 4 dpns. Join, being careful not to twist sts, and pm to denote beg of rnd.

Work 10 rnds of K2, P2 ribbing.

Switch to larger needles and knit 1 rnd.

Work rnds 1–4 of chart A once, then rep rnds 1and 2 once more.

Work all rows of chart B once, AT SAME TIME inc 1 (2, 2) sts on row 1 of chart and dec 1 (2, 2) sts on row 11 of chart.

Work chart A until leg measures 5½ (6, 6½)" or desired length to heel.

Heel

Change to C, K11 (13, 13) sts, turn. P22 (26, 26) sts. Place rem instep sts on a holder or leave on spare needle.

Heel Flap

Work back and forth on the 22 (26, 26) heel sts as follows:

Row 1 (RS): *Sl 1 pw wyib, K1, rep from * to end of row.

Row 2 (WS): Sl 1 pw wyif, purl to end of row.

Rep rows 1 and 2 until 22 (26, 26) rows are complete.

Heel Turn

Row 1 (RS): K13 (15, 15), ssk, K1, turn.

Row 2 (WS): Sl 1 pw, P5, P2tog, P1, turn.

Row 3: Sl 1 pw, knit to 1 st before gap, ssk (1 st before and 1 st after gap), K1, turn.

Row 4: Sl 1 pw, purl to 1 st before gap, P2tog (1 st before and 1 st after gap), P1, turn.

Rep rows 3 and 4 until all heel sts have been worked. End with row 4—14 (16, 16) sts rem.

Gusset

Change to A and arrange sts on 3 dpns as follows:

Needle 1: Knit across all 14 (16, 16) heel sts. With same needle, pick up 11 (13, 13) sts along side edge of heel flap.

Needle 2: Knit across held instep sts. (If you prefer working with a set of 5 dpns, you may divide these sts on 2 needles.)

Needle 3: Pick up 11 (13, 13) sts along side edge of heel flap. Knit across 7 (8, 8) heel sts from needle 1—58 (68, 68) sts. This is beg of rnd.

Return to knitting in the rnd and beg decs as follows:

Rnd 1 (dec rnd): On needle 1, knit to last 3 sts, K2tog, K1.

On needle 2, knit across all instep sts.

On needle 3, K1, ssk, knit to end—2 sts dec.

Rnd 2: Knit.

Rep rnds 1 and 2 until 44 (52, 52) total sts rem.

Foot

Work even in St st with A until foot measures 6½ (7½, 8)" or approx 2" shorter than desired foot length.

Toe

Change to C. Knit 1 rnd. Beg dec as follows:

Rnd 1 (dec rnd): On needle 1, knit to last 3 sts, K2tog, K1.

On needle 2, K1, ssk, work to last 3 sts on needle, K2tog, K1.

On needle 3, K1, ssk, knit to end—4 sts dec.

Rnd 2: Knit.

Rep rnds 1 and 2 until 16 sts rem.

FINISHING

Knit sts from needle 1 onto needle 3. Cut yarn, leaving an 8" tail. Close toe with kitchener st.

Weave in ends.

Kitchener Stitch

With yarn and darning needle,

1. Insert needle through first st on front as if to purl—leave on needle.

2. Insert needle through first st on back as if to knit—leave on needle.

3. Insert needle through first st on front as if to knit—remove from needle. Insert needle through next st on front as if to purl—leave on needle.

4. Insert needle through first st on back as if to purl—remove from needle. Insert needle into next st on back as if to knit—leave on needle

Repeat steps 3 and 4 until all sts have been worked. Fasten off and weave in end.

Chart A

Chart B

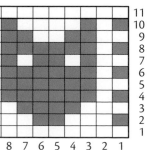

Color key

☐ Color A (white)
■ Color B (tan)
■ Color C (beige)

embroidered **baby blanket**

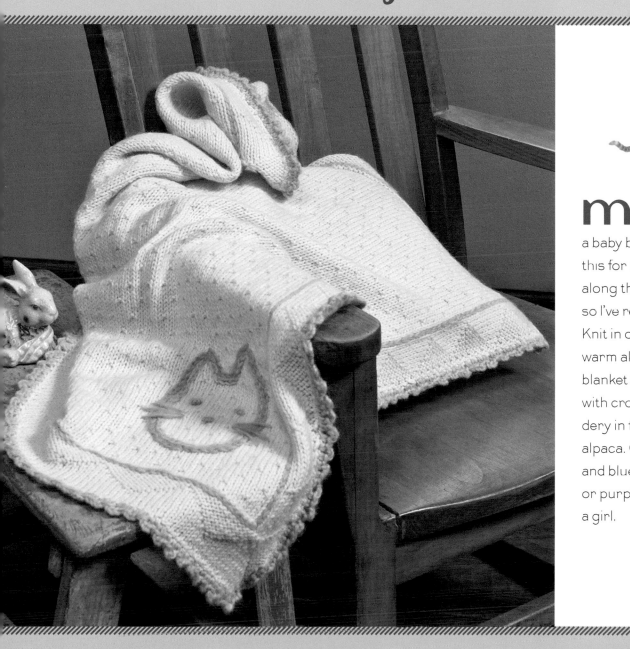

my mother made a baby blanket just like this for me. Somewhere along the way it got lost, so I've recreated it here. Knit in oh-so-soft and warm alpaca yarn, the blanket is embellished with crochet embroidery in fuzzy brushed alpaca. Choose green and blue trim for a boy or purple and pink for a girl.

55

SKILL LEVEL

Easy ●■□□

FINISHED MEASUREMENTS

Approx 30" wide x 30" long when blocked

MATERIALS

MC 8 balls of Suri Merino from Plymouth Yarn (55% Suri alpaca, 45% extra-fine merino; 109 yds; 50 g), color 100 **4**

A 1 ball of Baby Alpaca Brush from Plymouth Yarn (80% baby alpaca, 20% acrylic; 110 yds; 50 g), color 1620 **5**

B 1 ball of Baby Alpaca Brush from Plymouth Yarn, color 1620 **5**

Size 8 (5 mm) needles or size to obtain gauge

Stitch holders

Tapestry needle for sewing seams

Size H/8 (5 mm) crochet hook

GAUGE

20 sts = 4" in center patt (chart C)

INSTRUCTIONS

CO 141 sts.

Row 1 (RS): Knit.

Row 2 (WS): Purl.

Bottom Border

Beg chart A as follows:

Work sts 1–14 of chart A once, rep sts 15–28 a total of 8 times across row, work sts 29–43 once.

Work all rows of chart A.

Middle Patterns

Work 10 sts of chart B, pm, rep chart C 11 times across row, pm, work 10 sts of chart D.

Rep rows 1–14 of charts B and D until blanket measures approx 30". Work rows 15–20 of charts B and D once.

Top Border

Beg chart E on WS and work as follows:

Work sts 1–14 of chart E once, rep sts 15–28 a total of 8 times across row, work sts 29–43 once.

Work all rows of chart E.

Purl 1 row. BO on RS.

FINISHING

Weave in ends. Block blanket (see page 76 for blocking instructions).

With MC, work 1 row of sc around blanket, working 3 sts in each corner. Fasten off.

With A, work crochet edging as follows: *Sc in next 2 sts, ch 2, rep from * around entire edge of blanket.

Fasten off.

With A, work chain-st embroidery using needle or crochet hook (see page 77) around ridge just inside triangle edge.

With A and B, embroider design with crochet chain st following chart F.

Weave in crochet and embroidery ends, working them into areas of the same color.

If desired, lightly steam the crochet edging with an iron on medium heat.

Kitty Face

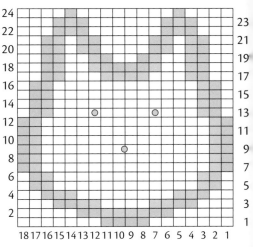

Key

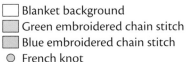

☐ Blanket background
Green embroidered chain stitch
Blue embroidered chain stitch
○ French knot

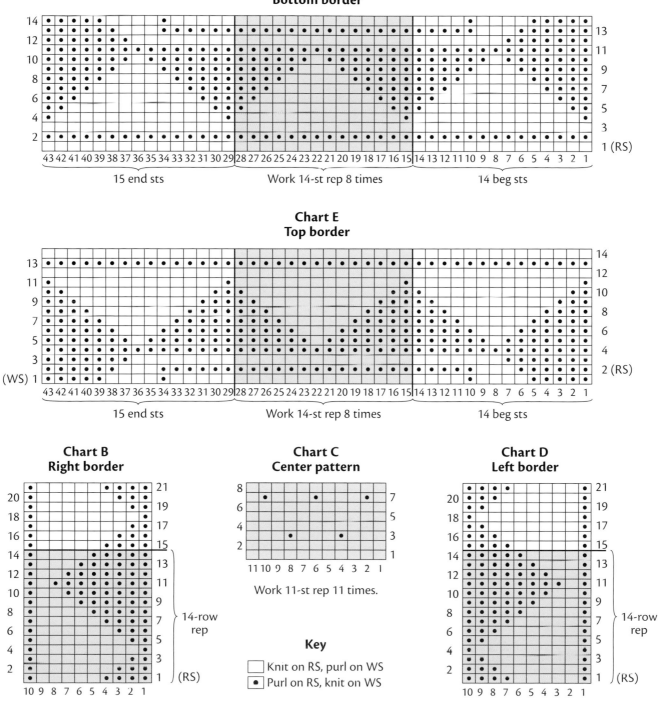

Chart A
Bottom border

15 end sts — Work 14-st rep 8 times — 14 beg sts

Chart E
Top border

15 end sts — Work 14-st rep 8 times — 14 beg sts

Chart B
Right border

14-row rep

Chart C
Center pattern

Work 11-st rep 11 times.

Chart D
Left border

14-row rep

Key

☐ Knit on RS, purl on WS
• Purl on RS, knit on WS

felted carpet **bag**

We knitters never have enough bags, do we? This bag is big enough to carry a good-sized knitting project and everything you need for a plane trip. It's knit in intarsia, felted, and embellished with needle felting.

SKILL LEVEL

Intermediate ■■■□

FINISHED MEASUREMENTS

Approx 24" wide x 14" tall (after felting)

Exact dimensions are determined during felting.

MATERIALS

Galway Worsted from Plymouth Yarn (100% wool; 210 yds; 100 g) **(4)**

A 5 balls of color 83 (pale blue)

B 2 balls of color 127 (pale green)

C 3 balls of color 8 (white)

D 2 balls of color 13 (purple)

E 20 yds of color 147 (yellow)

F 20 yds of color 154 (orange)

G 20 yds of color 135 (pink)

Size 9 (5.5 mm) needles or size to obtain gauge

2 size 9 double-pointed needles for handles

2 wooden 16"-long dowels, approx ¼" diameter

Tapestry needle

Heavy-duty felting needle, 38-gauge star point

Needle-felting mat

GAUGE

11 sts = 4" in St st using 2 strands of yarn held tog (before felting)

Exact gauge is not critical. Make sure your stitches are open and airy for felting.

STOCKINETTE STITCH

Knit RS rows, purl WS rows.

INSTRUCTIONS

Front

With 1 strand each of A and B held tog, CO 75 sts.

Row 1 (RS): Work row 1 of chart.

Cont in St st, work chart as est through row 28.

On row 29, cut B and add C to A. Cont as est until all 64 rows of chart have been completed.

Facing

Cut C. With 1 strand of A, K3, (K1f&b, K3) across—93 sts.

Work 7 rows of St st.

BO all sts.

Back

With A and B held tog, CO 75 sts.

Working in St st, work 28 rows.

On row 29, cut B and add C to A. Cont in St st until bag measures same height as front to start of facing.

Work facing as for front.

BO all sts.

Butterfly Rectangle

With 1 strand of G, CO 30 sts. Knit a St-st rectangle in random stripes using colors E, F, and G. When rectangle measures approx 8" high, BO all sts. You will cut this to shape after felting.

Handles (Make 6 Pieces)

With 1 strand each of A and C held tog and dpns, CO 3 sts. Work I-cord (see page 74) for 14". BO all sts.

Divide I-cord into 2 sets of 3 and make 2 braids. Sew the ends of the braids tog so they don't come apart during felting.

FINISHING

Sew front to back at sides and bottom, leaving sides of facing open. Fold facing to inside and stitch down hem, leaving ends open. Weave in ends on all pieces.

Felt all pieces according to instructions on page 76.

Fold the top 4" of the bag toward the inside, like a brown paper lunch bag.

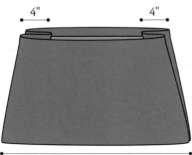

4"   4"

Approx 24" (after felting)

When pieces are completely dry, use needle felting to outline cat and smooth out edges.

Cut a butterfly shape out of the felted rectangle. Using the photo or your imagination as a guide, place the butterfly on top of the bag and put the needle-felting mat inside the bag. Using D, needle felt a body on the butterfly, going through both layers. This will attach the butterfly to the bag. Using the colors of your choice, needle felt circles or other designs on the butterfly wings.

Cut dowels to 1" shorter than the width of the top of the bag. Insert the dowels into the facing sleeve.

Sew handles to facing approx 4" from outside edges. Weave in rem ends.

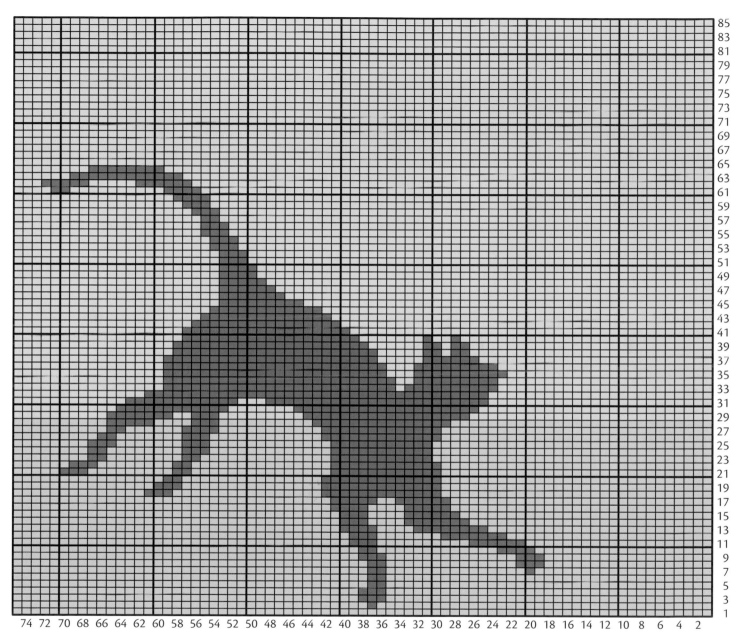

85
83
81
79
77
75
73
71
69
67
65
63
61
59
57
55
53
51
49
47
45
43
41
39
37
35
33
31
29
27
25
23
21
19
17
15
13
11
9
7
5
3
1

74 72 70 68 66 64 62 60 58 56 54 52 50 48 46 44 42 40 38 36 34 32 30 28 26 24 22 20 18 16 14 12 10 8 6 4 2

Color key

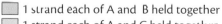 1 strand each of A and B held together
1 strand each of A and C held together
2 strands of D held together

felted appliqué **pillow**

this unique pillow front is knit in intarsia color work. The leaves, branches, and berries are made separately. Everything is felted, and then the decorations are sewn on as appliqués.

SKILL LEVEL

Intermediate ◼◼◼◻

FINISHED MEASUREMENTS

Approx 12" x 20" (after felting)

Exact gauge is determined during felting.

MATERIALS

Tweed from Plymouth Yarn (100% virgin lamb's wool; 109 yds; 50 g)
4

A 3 balls of color 5321 (navy blue)

B 3 balls of color 5316 (dark rose)

C 1 ball of color 5302 (cream)

D 20 yds of color 5306 (brown)

E 20 yds of color 5313 (orange)

F 20 yds of color 5314 (green)

G 20 yds of color 5315 (red)

H 20 yds of color 5325 (blue)

Size 9 (5.5 mm) needles or size to obtain gauge

Tapestry needle

Approx 2 yards of cotton scrap yarn

Sewing needle and navy blue thread

Pillow form or polyester fiberfill, size or amount to be determined by finished pillow

Tracing paper and Magic Marker (optional)

GAUGE

11 sts = 4" in St st (before felting)

Exact gauge is not critical. Make sure your stitches are open and airy for felting.

STOCKINETTE STITCH

Knit RS rows; purl WS rows.

INSTRUCTIONS

The front is worked in intarsia (see page 74) and the back in simple stripes.

Front

With A, CO 81 sts.

Work 3 rows in St st.

Next row (RS): Work 5 sts with A; working in intarsia with B and C, beg row 1 of chart on next 45 sts; work rem 31 sts with A.

Cont in St st in patt as est until all 89 rows of chart have been worked.

Work 4 rows in St st with A.

BO all sts.

Back

With A, CO 81 sts. Working in St st, work 2 rows in A and 2 rows in B until 96 rows have been worked. BO all sts.

Stems (Make 5 Stems)

With D, CO 3 sts. Work I-cord (see page 74) for desired length. BO all sts.

Make 1 stem at least 6" long, and 4 stems about 2" to 4" long.

Leaves

(Make 2 or 3 large and 2 or 3 small leaves in colors E, F, and G)

SMALL LEAF

CO 3 sts.

Row 1 (RS): K1, (YO, K1, YO), K1—5 sts.

Row 2 (and all WS rows): Purl.

Row 3: K2, (YO, K1, YO), K2—7 sts.

Row 5: K3, (YO, K1, YO), K3—9 sts.

Row 7: K4, (YO, K1, YO), K4—11 sts.

Row 9: Knit.

Row 11: K2tog, knit to last 2 sts, K2tog—9 sts.

Row 12: Purl.

Rep rows 11 and 12 until 3 sts rem.

K3tog. Fasten off.

LARGE LEAF

CO 3 sts.

Row 1 (RS): K1, (YO, K1, YO), K1—5 sts.

Row 2 (and all WS rows): Purl.

Row 3: K2, (YO, K1, YO), K2—7 sts.

Row 5: K3, (YO, K1, YO), K3—9 sts.

Row 7: K4, (YO, K1, YO), K4—11 sts.

Row 9: K5, (YO, K1, YO), K5—13 sts.

Row 11: K6, (YO, K1, YO), K6—15 sts.

Row 13: Knit.

Row 15: K2tog, knit to last 2 sts, K2tog—13 sts.

Row 16: Purl.

Rep rows 15 and 16 until 3 sts rem.

K3tog. Fasten off.

Berries (Make 12 to 15)

With G, put a slipknot on needle. Make a bobble as follows:

Row 1 (RS): (K1, P1, K1, P1, K1) in the slipknot—5 sts made. Turn.

Row 2: Purl 5. Turn.

Row 3: Knit 5. Turn.

Row 4: Purl 5. Turn.

Row 5: K1, K2tog, pass first st over as in binding off, K2tog, pass previous st over—1 st rem.

Fasten off.

Bird Rectangle

With H, CO 30 sts. Knit until piece measures approx 8". BO all sts.

FINISHING

Weave in ends on all pieces.

Sew front to back on sides and top. Sew bottom, leaving approx half of width open in center. Baste opening with cotton yarn.

Felt all pieces according to directions on page 76. Remove cotton basting and allow pieces to dry thoroughly.

Cut a bird shape out of blue rectangle you made. If you are not comfortable doing this freehand, trace the drawing onto tracing paper. Make pinholes in the drawing; then hold tracing over blue rectangle and transfer outline onto rectangle with Magic Marker. Or, make template of bird shape and trace around it with a marker. Be sure to cut inside of marker lines so they don't show.

Using the photo and your imagination as a guide, sew the various appliqué pieces to pillow.

Take pillow to a craft or fabric store and purchase a pillow form that will fit inside. If there is none of an appropriate size, buy a bag of fiberfill instead. Stuff pillow. Use the needle and thread to sew bottom closed. Fluff pillow into shape if necessary.

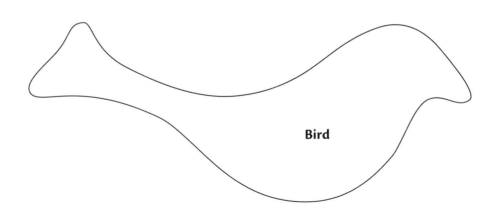

Bird

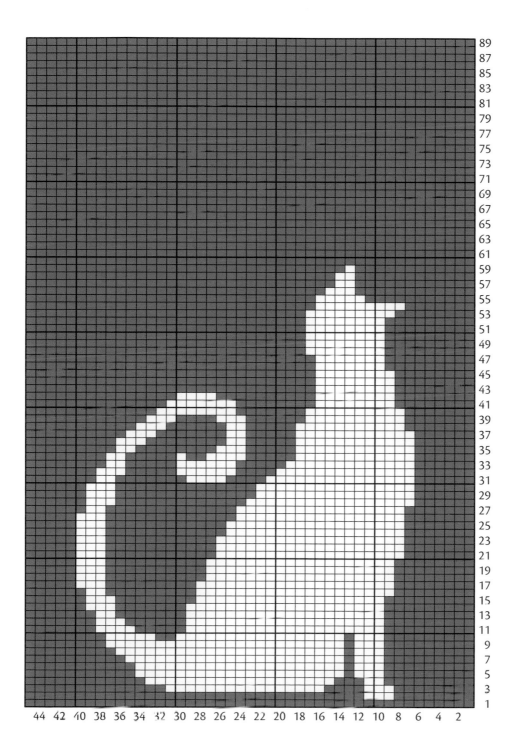

Color key

B (dark rose)

C (cream)

"the cat" afghan

a warm, bulky throw will keep you comfy while you curl up with a book or with your favorite cat. This throw is made on large needles in chunky yarn. The center is knit in an easy lace pattern. The words "The Cat" in several languages are embroidered around the edges using duplicate stitch.

SKILL LEVEL

Intermediate ◼◼◼◻

FINISHED MEASUREMENTS

Approx 46" x 46" (after blocking)

MATERIALS

Merino Supreme from Plymouth Yarn (100% merino wool; 64 yds; 50 g)
(5)

MC 22 balls of color 2226 (cream)

A 1 ball of color 2202 (gray)

B 1 ball of color 2205 (tan)

C 1 ball of color 2224 (brown)

D 1 ball of color 2210 (black)

Size 7 (4.5 mm) circular needle (at least 36" long) or size to obtain gauge

Stitch markers

Tapestry needle

GAUGE

20 sts and 5½ rows = 4" in lace patt

SEED STITCH

Worked over an even number of sts

Every row: (K1, P1) across.

INSTRUCTIONS

The borders are worked along with the center pattern.

Bottom Border

CO 186 sts.

Work 4 rows of seed st.

Next row (RS): Work 24 sts of seed st, pm, knit to last 24 sts, pm, work 24 sts of seed st.

Next row (WS): Work 24 sts of seed st, sm, purl to marker, sm, work 24 sts of seed st.

Rep last 2 rows another 9 times, slipping markers when you come to them, for a total of 20 rows of St st.

Center

Row 1 (RS): Work 4 sts of seed st, pm, K20, sm, work row 1 of diagonal lace patt over next 138 sts, sm, K20, pm, work 4 sts of seed st.

Row 2 (WS): Work 4 sts of seed st, sm, P20, sm, purl to next marker, sm, P20, sm, work 4 sts of seed st.

Work 39 repeats of diagonal lace patt. End after working row 6 of chart. Piece should measure approx 42" from beg of diagonal lace patt.

Top Border

Next row (RS): Work 24 sts of seed st, pm, knit to last 24 sts, pm, work 24 sts of seed st.

Next row (WS): Work 24 sts of seed st, sm, purl to marker, sm, work 24 sts of seed st.

Rep last 2 rows another 9 times, slipping markers when you come to them, for a total of 20 rows of St st.

Work 4 rows of seed st.

BO all sts.

FINISHING

Block afghan according to directions on page 76.

Add duplicate-stitch embroidery (see page 77) using photo and border charts as a guide. Lightly steam embroidery if desired.

Weave in ends.

Diagonal lace pattern

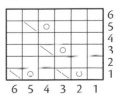

Stitch key

☐	Knit on RS, purl on WS
⊙	YO
╲	Ssk

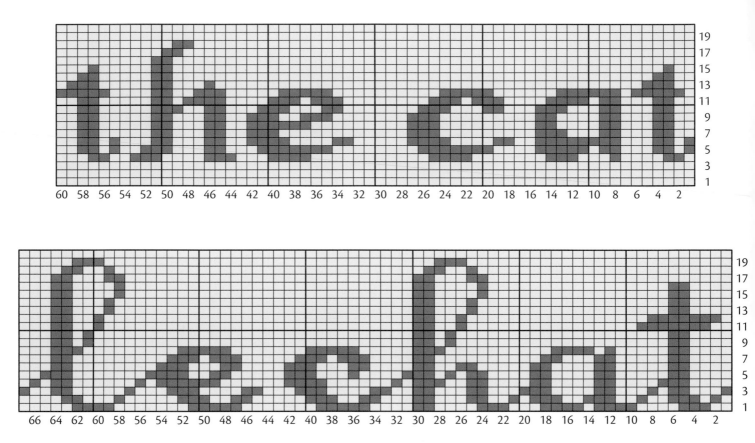

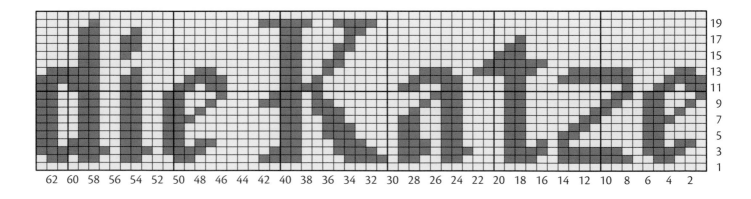

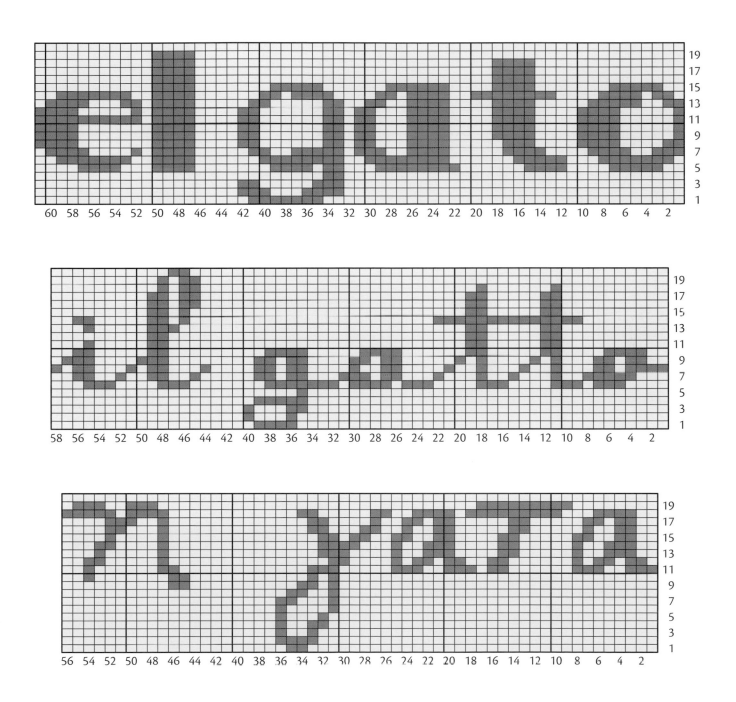

felted cat **doorstop**

this fun, felted feline friend is knit flat. The front and back are sewn together and a bottom is added for depth. The kitty is felted, the face is added by needle felting, and then the doorstop is stuffed with fiberfill. A water bottle filled with sand adds extra weight at the bottom.

SKILL LEVEL

Intermediate ◼◼◼▢

FINISHED MEASUREMENTS

Approx 18" tall (after felting)

Exact size is determined during felting.

MATERIALS

Galway Chunky from Plymouth Yarn (100% wool; 123 yds; 100 g) ⑤

A   5 balls of color 9 (black)

B   1 ball of color 702 (gray)

Size 13 (9) mm needles or size to obtain gauge

Tapestry needle

Heavy-duty felting needle, 38-gauge star point

Small needle-felting mat or small piece of Styrofoam

Polyester fiberfill for stuffing

1 pint water bottle

Sand

GAUGE

Approx 2¾ sts = 4" in St st using 2 strands of yarn held tog (before felting)

Exact gauge is not critical. Make sure your stitches are open and airy for felting.

GARTER STITCH

Knit every st in every row.

STOCKINETTE STITCH

Knit RS rows; purl WS rows.

REVERSE STOCKINETTE STITCH

Purl RS rows; knit WS rows.

INSTRUCTIONS

The front is worked in intarsia (see page 74) in St st and the back is worked in one color in rev St st.

Front

With 2 strands of A held tog, CO 15 sts.

Work cat-shaping chart in St st as follows:

Row 1 (RS): K15.

Row 2 (WS): CO 5, purl to end.

Row 3: CO 17, knit to end.

On rem rows, inc or CO to add sts at beg of each row or dec, or BO to remove sts at beg of each row as indicated on chart. Fasten off rem sts at tips of ears.

Back

With 2 strands of A held tog, CO 15 sts.

Work cat-shaping chart in rev St st as follows:

Row 1 (WS): P15.

Row 2 (RS): CO 5, knit to end.

Row 3: CO 17, purl to end.

On rem rows, inc or CO to add sts at beg of each row or dec, or BO to remove sts at beg of each row as indicated on chart. Fasten off rem sts at tips of ears.

Bottom

With 2 strands of B held tog, CO 35 sts. Knit 1 row.

Inc row: K1, M1, knit to end of row.

Rep inc row, working in garter st, until you have 45 sts.

Work even in garter st for 6".

Dec row: K2tog, knit to end of row.

Rep dec row, working in garter st, until you have 35 sts.

BO all sts.

FINISHING

Sew front to back around all edges except bottom. Sew bottom to doorstop, leaving at least 6" open.

Felt according to directions on page 76.

When piece is completely dry, put felting mat or Styrofoam inside of doorstop. Needle felt face and any other desired areas, using photo and your imagination as a guide.

Stuff doorstop with fiberfill. Fill a water bottle with sand and place it in the bottom of the doorstop for extra weight.

Sew the opening at the bottom of the doorstop closed.

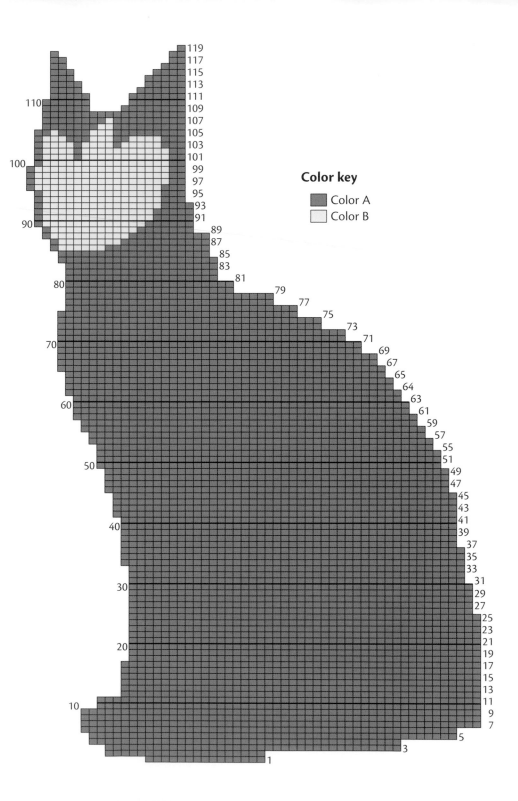

Color key

- Color A
- Color B

techniques

Basic knitting skills are all that is required to make most of the projects in this book. The projects are all identified with a skill level as defined below.

■□□□ **Beginner:** For all knitters. If you know how to knit, purl, cast on, and bind off, you have the required skills.

■■□□ **Easy:** For knitters who have made at least two or three projects. They may include some shaping, multiple colors, or easy stitch patterns.

■■■□ **Intermediate:** For knitters who have been around the block once or twice. They include shaping, circular knitting, color work, or more intricate pattern stitches, such as lace.

■■■■ **Experienced:** For adventurous knitters. They include unusual shaping techniques and complex pattern stitches that require your full attention.

KNITTING STITCHES AND TECHNIQUES

Refer to these stitches and techniques as needed for completing projects.

The following table identifies the yarn weights used in this book. Refer to this table when substituting yarns in a project.

STANDARD YARN-WEIGHT SYSTEM						
Yarn-Weight Symbol and Category Names	Super Fine **1**	Fine **2**	Light **3**	Medium **4**	Bulky **5**	Super Bulky **6**
Types of Yarns in Category	Sock, Fingering, Baby	Sport, Baby	DK, Light Worsted	Worsted, Afghan, Aran	Chunky, Craft, Rug	Bulky, Roving
Knit Gauge Ranges in Stockinette Stitch to 4"	27 to 32 sts	23 to 26 sts	21 to 24 sts	16 to 20 sts	12 to 15 sts	6 to 11 sts
Recommended Needle in U.S. Size Range	1 to 3	3 to 5	5 to 7	7 to 9	9 to 11	11 and larger
Recommended Needle in Metric Size Range	2.25 to 3.25 mm	3.25 to 3.75 mm	3.75 to 4.5 mm	4.5 to 5.5 mm	5.5 to 8 mm	8 mm and larger

Cable Cast On

The cable cast on can be used in place of any standard cast on (begin with step 1), or to add stitches to the beginning of a row (begin with step 3).

1. Make a slipknot about 4" from the end of the yarn. This is the first stitch.

2. Knit one stitch. Leave the slipknot on the left needle, and place the new stitch back on the left needle as well. You now have two stitches on the left needle.

3. Insert the right needle between the last two stitches on the left needle and wrap the yarn as if to knit.

4. Pull the yarn through.

5. Place the new stitch back on the left needle as shown below.

Repeat steps 3–5 for the required number of stitches.

Insert needle between two stitches. Knit a stitch.

Place new stitch on left needle.

I-Cord

I-cord is a long, thin tube of knitting, usually made on three or four stitches, and made using two double-pointed needles.

To knit I-cord:

1. With double-pointed needles, cast on the number of stitches instructed in the pattern, usually three or four. Do not turn. Slide the stitches to opposite end of the needle.

2. Knit all stitches. Do not turn.

3. Slide the stitches to opposite end of the needle.

Repeat steps 2 and 3 for the desired length. Bind off.

I-Cord Bind Off

I-cord can also be used to bind off a piece of knitting.

To attach I-cord to the edge of a piece of knitting that does not have live stitches, pick up stitches along the edge so you have live stitches. All of the stitches should be on the left needle.

1. Cast on four stitches at the end of the needle.

2. Knit three stitches. Then knit two stitches together through the back loop (one I-cord stitch and one stitch from the knitted piece). Do not turn.

3. Slip the four stitches back onto the left needle.

Repeat steps 2 and 3 for the desired length. Bind off.

Fair Isle (Stranded Color Work)

When knitting with two colors in a row and whenever you have more than five or six stitches of the same color, you should weave the unused color as you go. This prevents the yarns from tangling and creates a smooth, neat back for your knitting. For a fabric that will be felted, knit no more than two or three stitches without weaving the unused yarn. If you leave longer strands, or floats, on the back of your work, they may felt more than the other areas of the knitting, creating a puckered surface.

To weave in the unused color as you go:

1. Hold the working yarn in your right hand and the unused yarn in your left hand.

2. Bring the unused yarn over the right needle and knit a stitch with the working yarn, drawing it under the unused yarn as shown below.

3. Knit the next stitch normally with the working yarn, letting the unused yarn drop out of the way.

Continue to weave stitches as desired to eliminate long floats. The illustration below shows the unused yarn woven in on the wrong side of the work.

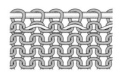

Intarsia (Color Blocks)

When knitting separate blocks of color, each color is worked with a separate ball of yarn. The yarns are crossed at the color change to lock the sections together. To work small motifs, wind off a small amount of yarn for each color area and let it hang loose at the back of your work.

To change colors in the middle of a row:

1. With the first color, knit up to the color change, then drop the first color.

2. Pick up the second color, crossing the yarn underneath the first color, and work the first stitch tightly. Give the end of the old color a slight tug to lock colors together.

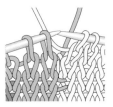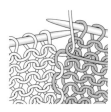

Right side of work   Wrong side of work

Lace

Knitted lace is made by combining yarn overs to create holes, with increases and decreases that draw lines and remove stitches. To work a yarn over:

1. Bring the yarn to the front of the work between the needles and then over the needle again to the back of the work to begin the next knit stitch.

2. On the next row, work the yarn over as a regular knit or purl stitch as indicated in the chart.

The types of decreases to be used will be specified on the lace chart.

Short Rows

A short row is simply a row that has fewer stitches than the full piece of knitting. Short rows are used to shape knitted pieces without increases or decreases.

Turning in the middle of the row leaves a small hole. The hole can be eliminated by wrapping the stitch at the turning point.

When instructions tell you to "wrap and turn":

1. Work to the turning point.

2. To wrap the stitch, first slip the next stitch onto the right needle. Then, bring the yarn to the front and slip the same stitch back to the left needle.

3. Turn the work and knit or purl the next stitch.

This technique creates a float on the right side of the work. On the next complete row, when you work back over the wrapped stitch, knit the wrap together with the corresponding stitch on the left-hand needle as shown above right.

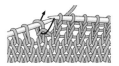

Right side of work

Wrong side of work

FINISHING TECHNIQUES

These techniques will ensure that your finished knitting projects look neat and professional.

Three-Needle Bind Off

The three-needle bind off is used to join two pieces of knitting together instead of sewing a seam. Both pieces must have the same number of stitches. To join knitted pieces with the three-needle bind off:

1. Place the two pieces on knitting needles so the right sides of each piece are facing each other with the needles parallel.

2. Insert a third needle through the first stitch on each needle as if to knit. Knit these stitches together as one, leaving one stitch on the right-hand needle.

3. Repeat step 2 and slip the older stitch on the left-hand needle over the newer stitch.

Repeat step 3 until all stitches are bound off.

Knit together one stitch from front needle and one stitch from back needle.

Bind off.

Blocking

Blocking is a washing and shaping technique used to make your item match the dimensions specified in the pattern and finishes the texture of the knitting, smoothing out any inconsistencies in gauge. By stretching the knitting, the yarn overs open up, the lace pattern becomes more visible and delicate, and the fabric obtains a beautiful drape.

To block an item:

1. Soak the finished item in tepid water until thoroughly wet, at least 1 hour. If desired, use a no-rinse wool-washing solution.

2. Gently roll the item in a towel to remove excess water.

3. Lay the item out on a blocking board or other flat surface, stretching it gently to the desired dimensions.

4. If the item does not hold its shape, pin the edges of the item to the blocking surface. Do not stretch or pin ribbing.

5. When the item is completely dry, remove the pins.

Felting

Felt is a thick, matted fabric created by treating yarns from certain natural animal fibers, such as 100% wool or a blend of wool and mohair, with heat and agitation. Machine-washable wool ("superwash"), cotton, silk, and man-made fibers will not felt, but can be used along with a strand of wool to create interesting textures.

When you knit for felting, your gauge should be very loose so you can see space between the stitches. To felt a knitted item:

1. Put the item in a zippered pillowcase (to catch the lint) and toss it in the washing machine. Set the machine for the smallest load size with hot wash and cold rinse, and add a very small amount of soap. If you are felting a small item, add an old pair of jeans for extra agitation.

2. Check the felting every five minutes. Some yarns will felt within the first few minutes, while others may take two or three cycles.

3. When the fibers are matted and you don't want the item to shrink any more, take it out and gently rinse it in tepid water in the sink or rinse and spin in the washing machine. Roll the item in a towel and squeeze out the excess water.

4. Shape as instructed in the pattern and allow the item to dry thoroughly.

Sewing Seams

For sewing sweaters, I use a variety of standard seams that can be learned from most knitting encyclopedias.

I use whipstitch seams to sew accessories and items that will be felted. To sew a whipstitch seam:

1. Hold the two pieces of knitting with the wrong sides together.

2. With a tapestry needle and matching yarn, use one smooth motion to catch the stitch on the edge of one piece of knitting and then catch a stitch on the other piece as shown below.

3. Continue along the seam, pulling gently on the yarn every 2" to close the seam.

EMBELLISHMENT TECHNIQUES

I used the following techniques to embellish many of the projects in this book.

Appliqué

Appliqué is a technique used to sew shapes that have been knit or felted onto the surface of a piece of knitting to add additional color and texture. You can sew the pieces on with matching yarn, thread, or invisible thread using invisible or decorative stitches.

Embroidery

Here are the embroidery stitches I've used for embellishing the projects in this book.

Duplicate stitch is used to create the cat motif on the Ballet Cardigan and the words on "The Cat" Afghan. Because each stitch "duplicates" a knit stitch, it looks like the design was knit in.

I used French knots to make eyes and noses on the catnip mice.

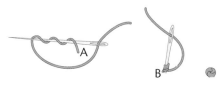

Satin stitch is used on the Felted Stuffed Cat's nose. Use straight stitches to fill in large solid areas.

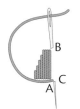

An embroidered chain stitch is used to create the cat face on the Embroidered Baby Blanket. This stitch looks like a crochet chain lying across the surface of the fabric. It can be made with an embroidery needle or a corchet hook.

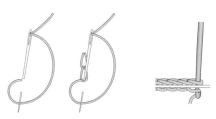

Needle Felting

Needle felting is a way to draw designs with wool on a piece of felted knitting without sewing. To apply needle felting:

1. Make sure the piece is thoroughly dry. Place the felted piece on the foam needle-felting surface.

2. Cut pieces of worsted-weight wool yarn 6" to 12" long. Place them on the felted piece, forming designs as instructed in the pattern.

3. With the felting needle, stab the yarn repeatedly until it becomes attached to the background. (Be careful; the felting needle is quite sharp and has a barbed edge.)

Crochet Embellishments

Chain stitch is used to create a foundation for crochet, just like casting on in knitting. To make a crochet chain:

1. Make a slipknot and place on hook.

2. Holding the crochet hook in your right hand and the yarn in your left hand, bring the yarn over the hook from front to back, turning the hook slightly to keep the yarn on the hook. Draw the yarn through the slipknot.

Repeat step 2 until the chain is the desired length.

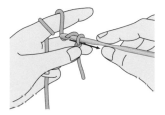

Single crochet makes a smooth edge that looks like the bind-off edge of knitting. To work a row of single crochet on the edge of a knitted piece:

1. Insert a crochet hook into a stitch on the edge of the knitting and draw a loop through to the front. Wrap the yarn around the hook and draw a second loop through the first to secure.

2. Working from right to left, insert the crochet hook into the next stitch on the edge of the knitting.

3. Pull the working yarn through to the front. Two loops are now on the hook.

4. Pull the working yarn through both loops on the hook. One loop remains on the hook.

Repeat steps 2–4 around the entire edge.

Insert hook into stitch, yarn over hook, pull loop through to front, yarn over hook.

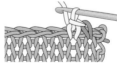

Pull loop through both loops on hook.

Crab stitch, also known as *reverse single crochet* because it is worked in the opposite direction, creates a decorative beaded edge. To work a row of crab stitch:

1. Insert a crochet hook into a stitch on the edge of the piece and draw a loop through to the front. Wrap the yarn around the hook and draw a second loop through the first to secure.

2. Working from left to right, insert the crochet hook into the next stitch.

3. Pull the working yarn through to the front. Be careful not to pull it through the loop already on the hook. Two loops are now on the hook.

4. Pull the working yarn through both loops on the hook. One loop remains on the hook.

Repeat steps 2–4 around the entire edge.

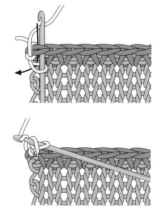

Tassels

A basic tassel is made from of a cluster of yarn, fastened at one end.

1. Cut a piece of cardboard ½" longer than the finished tassel.

2. Wrap yarn around the cardboard 25 times or until it's as full as you like.

> **Note:** Only half of the tassel is on one side of the cardboard; it will be twice as thick when finished.

3. Thread a 6" piece of yarn between the cardboard and the yarn loops and tie a knot. Use these tails to sew on the tassel.

4. Slip the loops off the cardboard.

5. Bind the tassel near the top, just below the hanging loop as follows: Wrap a 10" piece of yarn around the top of the tassel several times about ½" from the top. Thread both tails in a needle and hide them in the center of the tassel.

6. Cut open the bottom loops and trim the ends evenly.

abbreviations and glossary

approx	approximately
beg	begin(ning)
BO	bind off
CC	contrasting color
ch	chain
CO	cast on
cont	continue, continuing
dec(s)	decrease(s), deceasing (see also *K2tog, K2tog tbl,* and *ssk*)
dpn	double-pointed needle
est	established
g	grams
garter st	garter stitch; back and forth: knit every row; in the round: knit 1 round, purl 1 round
inc(s)	increase(s), increasing (see also *K1f&b* and *M1*)
K	knit
K1b	Knit 1 stitch through the back loop to make a twisted stitch
K1f&b	knit 1 stitch front and back: knit the stitch normally but do not drop the old stitch from the left needle; then knit the same stitch through the back loop and drop the old stitch (1 stitch increased)

K2tog	knit 2 together: insert the needle into 2 stitches at the same time and work them together as 1 stitch (1 stitch decreased, right slanting)
K2tog tbl	knit 2 together through the back loop: insert the needle into the back of 2 stitches at the same time and work them together as 1 stitch (1 stitch decreased, left slanting)
kw	knitwise
LH	left hand
M1	make 1 stitch: lift horizontal strand between the needles from front to back and place on left-hand needle; knit through back loop of stitch formed (1 stitch increased)
MC	main color
oz	ounces
P	purl
patt(s)	pattern(s)
pm	place marker
psso	pass slipped stitch(es) over
PU	pick up and knit
pw	purlwise
rem	remain(ing)
rep	repeat

RH	right hand
rnd(s)	round(s)
RS	right side(s)
sc	single crochet
sl	slip
sm	slip marker
ssk	slip, slip, knit: slip the next 2 stitches, one at a time, to the right needle as if to knit, then insert the left needle into the front of the stitches and knit the 2 stitches together as 1 stitch (1 stitch decreased, left slanting)
st(s)	stitch(es)
St st	stockinette stitch; back and forth: knit RS rows and purl WS rows; in the round: knit every round
tbl	through the back loop
tog	together
wyib	with yarn in back
wyif	with yarn in front
WS	wrong side
yds	yards
YO	yarn over

resources

All yarns were generously provided by Plymouth Yarn Company. Visit www.plymouthyarn.com.

The embellishments and finishing supplies used in this book are readily available in most craft and hobby shops.

about the author

Donna Druchunas grew up learning many different crafts from her mother and grandmothers, including knitting, crocheting, rug hooking, embroidering, and sewing. After a 25-year vacation from crafts, she started knitting again and learned to spin and dye wool with natural dyes. Before returning to knitting, Donna spent almost 20 years working in corporate cubicles as a writer, designer, and creative-services manager. Her cubes were in military-training facilities, small businesses, and large corporations.

After all that time, she rebelled and left her cubicle behind to combine her interest in knitting with her skill at writing easy-to-follow instructions. Donna's designs and articles have been featured in *Family Circle Easy Knitting, Knitters, Piecework, Interweave Knits, Fibre Focus,* and *INKnitters* magazines, and she designs patterns for several yarn companies. This is her fourth book.

Donna was born in New York City, but today she lives in the foothills of the Colorado Rocky Mountains with her husband and two cats, who are very helpful when it comes to testing new knitting designs!